T0339295

Into Wild Mongolia

INTO
WILD
MONGOLIA

■ ■ ■

GEORGE B. SCHALLER

Yale

UNIVERSITY PRESS

New Haven and London

Published with assistance from the Charles S. Brooks Publication Fund.

Published with assistance from the foundation established in memory of Amasa Stone Mather of the Class of 1907, Yale College.

Yale University Press books may be purchased in quantity for educational, business, or promotional use. For information, please e-mail sales.press@yale.edu (U.S. office) or sales@yaleup.co.uk (U.K. office).

Set in Adobe Garamond type by Tseng Information Systems, Inc.
Printed in the United States of America.

Library of Congress Control Number: 2019940797
ISBN 978-0-300-24617-9 (hardcover : alk. paper)

A catalogue record for this book is available from the British Library.
This paper meets the requirements of ANSI/NISO Z39.48-1992 (Permanence of Paper).

10 9 8 7 6 5 4 3 2 1

To the Mongolians who with dedication strive to
preserve the natural beauty of their country

Contents

Color plates follow page 82

A Note on Weights and Measures

1 inch = 2.54 centimeters (cm)
1 centimeter = 0.39 inches (in.)
1 foot = 0.305 meters (m)
1 meter = 3.28 feet
1 mile = 1.6 kilometers (km)
1 kilometer = 0.62 miles
1 square mile = 2.59 square kilometers (km^2)
1 square kilometer = 0.386 square miles (sq. miles)
1 acre = 0.40 hectares (ha)
1 hectare = 2.47 acres
1 pound = 0.454 kilograms (kg)
1 kilogram = 2.2 pounds (lbs.)
1 U.S. gallon = 3.78 liters
1 liter = 0.264 U.S. gallons (gals.)
Celsius to Fahrenheit: multiply by 1.8 and add 32
Fahrenheit to Celsius: subtract 32 and divide by 1.8

Note: Equivalences may vary depending on whether the conversion is from imperial to metric or metric to imperial and on how many decimals are included.

Into Wild Mongolia

Introduction

Thus shall you think of this fleeting world:
A star at dawn, a bubble in a stream,
A flash of lightning in a summer cloud,
A flickering lamp, a phantom, and a dream.

Gautama Buddha, Diamond Sutra

The train leaves Beijing at 7:40 a.m. on its thirty-hour journey to Ulaan Baatar, Mongolia's capital. The coach is crowded with Mongolians going home, all with large bags and bundles of goods for their households or to sell. Kay and I would have preferred going by plane, but there is only one flight a week. We are eager to leave Beijing. Today is August 12, 1989. It's been a little over two months since the "June Fourth Incident" on Tiananmen Square, when the military quelled student-led demonstrations for democracy, freedom of speech, and economic reform with a massacre of hundreds. Beijing is still under martial law. Military vehicles patrol the streets. And people remain apprehensive.

The train heads west past the Great Wall, built around 300 BCE to keep out raiding Mongolians and other northern hordes. (The word *horde* comes from the Mongolian *ordu*.) The route goes over plains and low hills covered with fields of maize and sunflowers to the town of Datong. From there we head north into China's Inner

Mongolia, showing the location of adjoining Russia and provinces of China.

Mongolia Autonomous Region. Wheat fields soon give way to sandy plains sparsely covered with grass. An occasional round felt-covered yurt, or ger, as it is called by Mongolians, seems lost in the vastness of the scene. Inner Mongolia is three-quarters the size of Mongolia but with a human population of 21 million, compared to about 2 million in Mongolia. A 1915 treaty between Russia and China divided the region into Inner Mongolia and Outer Mongolia, with China ruling the former and trying to remain overlord of the latter. However, Outer Mongolia proclaimed its independence in 1921, shedding the word *Outer.* China recognized Mongolia in 1946, and the following year the Inner Mongolia Autonomous Region was officially established.

When I was asked the previous year by the National Geographic Society if I would like to survey the wildlife of Mongolia, I naturally said yes. I had been working in China with local colleagues since 1980, first on a study of giant pandas and then on the uplands of the Tibetan Plateau on such species as wild yaks and Tibetan antelopes. Mongolia, an Alaska-sized country of 604,247 square miles (1,565,000 km², three times the size of France), squeezed between China and Russia, has wildlife that intrigues me. There are wild Bactrian (two-humped) camels, khulan (Mongolian wild asses), Mongolian gazelles, Gobi bears, and others, none of which had been studied in detail. Roy Chapman Andrews, in his 1932 study *The New Conquest of Central Asia,* describes the discovery of dinosaur eggs in 1923 and some of his encounters with wildlife, such as Mongolian gazelles: "The entire horizon appeared to be a moving line of yellow bodies and curving necks. . . . Nowhere else, except in Africa, would it be possible to see such a herd of wild animals. We estimated at least six thousand immediately in front of us, but there may have been twice that number."

How could I resist a visit to Mongolia?

Working in Mongolia might, however, present certain problems. China and Russia had for centuries juggled for power over the region. The years from the 1920s into the 1980s have been times of turmoil. Mongolia's capital was attacked by Chinese troops in 1919 and occupied in early 1920. Then in October 1920, just as Mongolia was trying to establish itself as an independent country, it was invaded by an army of so-called White Russians who were escaping Lenin's Bolsheviks. This army was led by Baron von Ungern-Sternberg, the "Mad Baron," a murderous, sadistic individual. His army conquered the capital, drove out the Chinese, and devastated the population. A witness later wrote, as quoted in Jasper Becker's *The Lost Country,* that for three days "innumerable men, women and children of all ages, races, and creeds were hacked to bits and bayoneted and shot and strangled and hanged and crucified and burnt alive." In 1921 joint Mongolian-Soviet forces chased the White Russians out, the Mad Baron was executed, and Mongolia proclaimed its independence.

In 1924 Mongolia adopted a Soviet-style constitution, the first country after the Soviet Union to become Communist. It became, in effect, a satellite of Russia. This alliance made Mongolia wholly dependent on Russia for trade and development, and the government had to follow the dictates of Stalin and his successors. Foreign contacts ruptured; the country walled itself in. The land of the great twelfth-century conquerors Genghis Khan and Kublai Khan had wound up totally subjected.

Would I get permission as an American to collaborate with Mongolian biologists? Things looked promising. The United States had opened an embassy in Ulaan Baatar in 1987. That same year Mongolia established its Ministry of Nature and Environment. (The ministry's name has undergone a number of changes, but for clarity I'll refer to it this way throughout.) And in 1989, the year the Iron Curtain was torn apart, Mongolia initiated what it called *il tod,* an opening to the world.

In 1988 I had applied to the new ministry for an invitation and was awaiting a reply when, without warning, the National Geographic Society canceled the proposed project. But the New York Zoological Society (later renamed the Wildlife Conservation Society), on whose staff I was a field biologist, continued to support me. To my delight, Kay and I received an official invitation from the ministry for Mongolia.

On August 13, 1989, our train reached Ehrenhot on the Mongolian border, where the wheels of the train have to be changed for a narrower gauge of track. After a three-hour halt we continue through the night, Kay and I dozing intermittently. Vast views of rolling rangelands greet the morning. Toward noon we enter hills and a valley sparsely covered with spruce, larch, and birch, and at 1:15 p.m. we arrive in sprawling Ulaan Baatar (also spelled Ulan Bator, or simply referred to as UB). The name means "red hero," and the city was renamed in 1924 in honor of the revolutionary hero Damdin Sukhbaatar, who died in 1923. The old name of the city since 1639 had been Urga.

G. Dembereldorj, the head of the foreign office of the Ministry of Nature and Environment, meets us. Dressed in a suit, he is lean and suave, and speaks excellent English. We drive to the center of town, past endless nondescript apartment blocks, to the Ulan Bator Hotel. A statue of Lenin stands before it. Massive Russian-style government buildings with Doric columns are nearby, including the Great Khural, the equivalent of the Supreme Soviet. Dembereldorj is refreshingly direct as we eat lunch. "What do you want to do? Where do you want to go? I will make the arrangements."

From my preliminary reading, I know that Mongolia is divided into four broad vegetation belts. In the south, toward China, is desert and semi-desert. In the middle is a broad band of grassland or steppe. And in the mountains to the north toward the Russian border are forests. I am drawn to desert and steppe, where I can observe animals at a distance, and where such species as wild camels and Mongolian gazelles attract me. But I wonder whether Mongolian scientists are already studying these and other species; the University of Ulaan Baatar was founded in 1942 and the Mongolian Academy of Sciences in 1961. Russians from various institutes have made surveys and collected specimens. And since 1962, Mongolian-German expeditions organized by the Martin Luther University in Halle, East Germany, have done much research, from beetles to beavers and from lice to lichens, and published hefty volumes of reports. I know from experi-

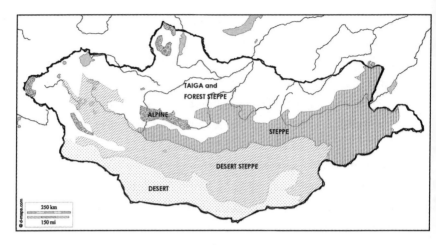

The main vegetation belts of Mongolia.
Our research focused on the steppe and desert.

ence elsewhere that biologists tend to be quite territorial, especially with regard to foreigners who might intrude on their species or area of study. Well, I would soon find out.

We decide that as a first step in our collaboration we will go to the Gobi desert to observe wild Bactrian camels and possibly Gobi bears. Both are found only in and around Great Gobi National Park, Part A, a Strictly Protected Area of 17,000 square miles (44,000 km²), extending southward to the border with China. Part B lies 150 miles to the west and is 3,400 square miles (8,800 km²). Little did I realize that in the following years I would return to Mongolia again and again, a total of sixteen trips between 1989 and 2007, each time for a month or two, to assist the country with its conservation of wildlife, and always anticipating with pleasure my return. After that, projects in India, Brazil, China, and others diverted my attention, but in 2018, after a decade of absence, I returned once more, eager to renew acquaintances and note changes in the environment, wildlife, and culture.

Both camels and bears are rare, though precise numbers are unknown. The Russian expeditions in the early 1980s had estimated about 650 wild camels and 25 to 30 Gobi bears. I wanted to learn more about the daily lives of these animals, having had experience with their relatives. Two years previously, my son Mark and I had crossed the Kunlun Mountains in China's Xinjiang region by camel caravan onto the Tibetan Plateau. There were nine Han Chinese and Uyghurs, in addition to Mark and me, and sixteen camels. I enjoy the gentle rocking back and forth when sitting between the two humps of a camel and seemingly floating through the silent mountain wasteland, the only sound the scuffing of the camel's footpads on sand and the clanging of a bell on the neck of the last camel in the caravan. Traveling through landscape slowly greatly appeals to me. However, this time we will have to go by noisy vehicles. As to bears, I have studied giant pandas and Asiatic black bears in China and also encountered the Tibetan brown bear there, all living in rather benign habitats. Yet here the Gobi bear persists in a harsh desert. How does it manage to survive?

Between June 1980 and October 1982, a Russian expedition conducted a detailed ecological survey in the Gobi. I have read the report, *The Great Gobi National Park: A Refuge for Rare Animals of the Central Asian Deserts,* by L. V. Zhirnov and V. O. Ilyinsky, which offers valuable information and stimulated me to delve deeper into the lives of the Gobi animals.

We have to wait four days while preparations for our trip are being made. I do not yet realize how difficult it is to obtain food, gasoline, functional vehicles, and other essentials. Meanwhile I wander around town near the Tuula River, sometimes with Kay and other times alone. In the center is the huge Sukhbaatar Square, where the Mongolian People's Republic was proclaimed, dominated by a statue of Damdin Sukhbaatar astride a prancing horse, his right arm raised. The mausoleum of Khorloogiin Choibalsan, the Stalinist dictator of the country for much of the first half of this century, is there too. I find it a strange juxtaposition: the country's liberator next to the body of the instigator of its Great Terror. The opera house, also on the square, is a typical Russian monolith in construction, and it displays large red banners of Lenin. Nearby is a statue of Stalin. The streets are broad but have little traffic, not even bicycles, as one would see in China. People walk. A pall from a huge coal-burning power plant hangs over the city with its half-million inhabitants, a quarter of the country's population. Walking along, I occasionally notice a man in a suit casually following me. If I stop to glance in a store window, he does too. Public security is keeping an eye on us, as it does on the rest of the population, ensuring cowed uniformity throughout the country. We look into a department store crowded with locals as well as Russian advisers and soldiers. But merchandise is scarce. One long line of people waits stoically at the children's clothing department, another at a bakery. One store accepts foreign exchange, but it sells mostly cigarettes and alcohol. When we are downtown the size of the city is not apparent. Thousands of people live crowded in yurts or gers in suburbs spread across nearby valleys and up on the slopes, most households secluded behind board fences without running water or sanitation.

During meetings at the ministry, I encounter several of my new colleagues. Jachliin Tserendeleg, the executive director of the Mongolian Society for Environment and Nature, is a delightfully enthusiastic individual in his late forties with twinkling eyes who is truly dedicated to helping the project. S. Chuluunbaatar, called Chuka, also works with a local conservation organization; he is in his thirties and speaks good English as well as German (he spent six years in

East Germany). Gol Amarsanaa is Mongolia's snow leopard biologist from the Academy of Sciences; also in his thirties, he is a stocky, Slavic-looking man who somewhat reluctantly agrees that he will work with us.

Dembereldorj and Tserendeleg—acquaintances here are usually addressed by their last name or nickname, not their given name—want to show us the remains of ancient culture in the city. We go to the so-called summer palace, the former home of the Jebtsundamba Hutukhtu, the Buddhist religious leader, third in the hierarchy of the Gelugpa sect after the Dalai Lama and Panchen Lama. Inside are some thangkas (wall hangings of religious scenes) and figures of Buddha. But my main impression is of a dead zoo. There are skins of tigers and snow leopards and a ger covered with leopard skins. One room is full of stuffed animals: a polar bear, a giraffe, penguins, a howler monkey, birds of paradise, and others. The Hutukhtu is said to have had a private zoo. He certainly leaves a most peculiar legacy. Indeed the "palace" is a monument to extinction, that of the Hutukhtu himself.

As a result of Mongol rule over parts of the Tibetan Plateau in the thirteenth and fourteenth centuries, Tibetan Buddhism of the Gelugpa, or Yellow, Sect became widespread throughout China and Mongolia, and in the latter it had become the principal religion by the sixteenth century. The convoluted history at this time was well described by Gavin Hambly in his *Central Asia:* "It was perhaps a combination of missionary zeal and political acumen which took the Third Dalai Lama, Sonam Gyatso (1543–88) to Mongolia where in 1578 he converted Altan Khan [a descendant of Genghis Khan] who first gave him the title of Dalai Lama which all his subsequent incarnations have held. Thereafter the Gelugpa sect spread rapidly in Mongolia, assisted by the foundation of numerous lamaseries (Erdeni Dzu, near Qaraquorum, was founded in 1586). Equally rapidly appeared that peculiar feature of Tibetan Buddhism in Mongolia—the proliferation of incarnations known as *khutukhtus.*" Conversion to Buddhism may have helped to give Mongolians a cultural identity, but it did not reduce their aggressiveness; tribal warfare and attacks on neighbors continued unabated.

We are now in the home of the last Hutukhtu, who is reputed to have been dissolute. He ruled for forty-nine years, the last thirteen as head of both church and state. The golden roofs of a hundred temples shimmered then in and around the city, and the chants of some fifteen thousand monks could be heard. He died in 1924. At that time the spiritual roots that bound Mongolians to Tibet began to dissolve.

The reincarnation of the Hutukhtu would no doubt be horrified with the city of 1989. His palace is a museum. The many temples and monasteries and monks are gone, vanished. As C. R. Bawden in *The Modern History of Mongolia* writes: "Practically nothing remains in Ulan Bator to suggest that it lies on the site of the old Urga, the centre of Mongol lamaism and once a rival in artistic splendour to Lhasa." Only the Gandan monastery, with about a hundred elderly monks, remains, as I saw during a brief visit. The rest was destroyed during a reign of terror in the 1920s and 1930s, an orgy of Soviet-inspired purges and massacres with a passion for destruction that wholly changed the culture of Mongolia. I knew few details about these past events during this first visit. When I gave a talk to my collaborating institutions about my work in Tibet, I included not just wildlife but many photos of the beautiful monasteries, colorful processions of monks, and religious festivals with large crowds being blessed by high-ranking lamas. My audience was uneasily fascinated in a way I had never noted during a lecture before. Was it a vague remembrance or denial of an appalling past, a pact of forgetting? Well, every nation invents its own history.

Books about Mongolia have usually focused on Genghis Khan and the tumultuous centuries following his conquests or on recent history, travelogues, and expedition accounts. Some of these books briefly mention wildlife. There are also many scientific papers about the various wildlife species by Mongolians, Russians, and biologists of other nationalities. But there is little popular literature by someone like myself, a naturalist who enjoys watching the behavior of animals and with compassion strives for their conservation. Of course, my colleagues and I also collected detailed data about the various species. For example, we placed radio-collars on snow leopards, Gobi bears, and Mongolian gazelles to track their movements and monitor their activities, the first time this had been done in Mongolia. Having such information about the habits of a species makes it possible for environmentalists and government agencies to prepare solid plans for its protection and management. Our work coincided with a particularly traumatic time for Mongolia, when it shifted from Russian totalitarianism through a period of "restructuring" in 1989–1992, and on to a more stable society. Vandalism, robbery, shortage of goods, and a changed boundary of ethics created an aura of apprehension and melancholy. Our studies at a time of such widespread tribulation offer an interesting historical perspective, one worthy of record, and in this book I attempt to convey it, based on my observations and experiences. However, to study nature has always been my main objective, in Mongolia and elsewhere, and other matters are mentioned mainly because they intruded on my vision.

I felt privileged to spend these years in Mongolia, and was fortunate that Minister Zamba Batjargal and Jachliin Tserendeleg generously hosted me. Many Mongolian biologists and local officials, who will make their appearance in the text, showed me, an itinerant American, a wonderful spirit of cooperation. Mongolian herders and other families are widely known for their hospitality, and we, mere strangers, were deeply grateful to be taken into their homes.

Since I was also committed to projects in other countries, I could only devote a limited time to Mongolia. I helped to establish various projects and then turned these over to others, both Mongolians and foreigners. I was fortunate in being able to include two excellent American field biologists in the work. One was Thomas McCarthy, who continued the studies on snow leopards, camels, and Gobi bears for several years, living in the country with his family. The other was Kirk A. Olson, who for over two decades has devoted himself mainly to the great eastern steppes and the Mongolian gazelles. With great dedication he is concerned about the conservation of this magnificent grassland, whose future is threatened by development, and he has also found personal fulfillment in the country, having married and settled there.

1

Wild Camels of the Gobi

Such a journey as the one we have just mentioned, besides its geographical interest, would finally set at rest the question of the existence of wild camels and horses. The natives repeatedly told us of the existence of both, and described them fully.

Nikolay Przhevalsky, 1879

We have agreed that the focus of this trip to Great Gobi National Park in August and September 1989 will be to gather detailed information on the wild camels, and only incidentally on other species. I am impatient to leave for the field, to see and feel the desert, to take my binoculars and wander across the landscape, to watch the private life of camels. Meetings, discussions, preparations, waiting, and more waiting consume days. Finally on August 18, Chuka, Kay, and I fly west to the town of Altai. The two-hour flight passes over forested ridges, the highest peaks snow covered. After checking into a hotel, we wander around the small town of low buildings and barracks and a ger suburb. A large sign in Russian Cyrillic script proclaims, "Herds are our wealth." (Since the 1990s, with the new "openness," the old Mongolian script has, I'm told, been making a cautious comeback.) Posters of Lenin and large red stars adorn buildings. I look into a shop. The shelves are bare except for some shoes and toothpaste.

We leave in two Russian jeeps on the 155 mile (250 km) drive across rolling grassland to Gobi Park. Three demoiselle cranes watch us pass. I have seen many of these cranes nesting in the wetlands of the Tibetan Plateau, and then migrating over the Himalayas south to Nepal and India for the winter. I wonder where these three will spend the cold months. While crossing a low mountain range, I tally a number of chunky marmots, dark gray and tan in color. They are survivors. Mongolia has been exporting many thousand marmot skins annually to Russia. Ground squirrels sit bolt upright, alertly monitoring us, and then bound to their burrows, white-tipped tails flowing behind them. After traversing another ridge, we descend into a broad valley dotted with soda lakes and bypass a county town known as a *soum, somon,* or *sum* in the local language. At the next range, by a small waterfall and a clear stream we stop for lunch—bread, cucumbers, and canned mutton spread, the last-named only obtainable from special army supply stores. On the grass slopes of yet another range are large herds of black-faced, fat-tailed sheep. At a 7,875-foot (2,400 m) pass is a cairn, or *oboo,* of pebbles surmounted by several old ibex and argali sheep horns and rusty car parts. We stop and add a pebble to the cairn, a Buddhist ritual signifying our devotion to giving.

After descending into a large outwash plain, we stop at a ger. The family is raising four wild-caught baby camels with domestic foster mothers for a government captive-breeding program. These baby *khavtgai,* as the wild camel is here called, were born the previous spring. They are endearing animals, light gray-brown in color, with spindly legs, two tiny humps topped with a tuft of dark hair, and bulging soft eyes. Last year two of five captured young died. Why do the herders need to capture the young at all? I hope to find out.

Ten hours after leaving Altai we reach Bayan Tooroi, the headquarters of Great Gobi National Park, located over a mile outside the park. It is a sprawling place with about twenty brick bungalows and

Principal protected areas in Mongolia mentioned in the text.

several dozen gers. A line of massive, gnarled cottonwoods (*Populus*) traces an underground stream. The branches have an abrupt browse line about nine feet (2.7 m) above ground, the height a camel can reach. Our room is stark, with two beds, a hat stand, and many flies. There is also a refrigerator, and I open it. Inside are large chunks of bloody, rotting meat.

The park director, U. Chuluun, short, stocky, and congenial, stops by to greet us and informs us that he will prepare a truck with gasoline, food, and other items we will need for two weeks in the park. Ravdangiin Tulgat also introduces himself. He has been in charge of research in the park for the past six years. Tall and lean, he has a rather glum face but wears a condescending smile, as if contemplating a private joke. As our guide on the trip, he will, I hope, teach me much about camels and other wildlife.

Dawn is at seven, but no one even begins to stir before eight. I soon learn that our Mongolian colleagues have a great capacity for sleeping late into the morning, whereas Kay and I are usually up early.

At 11:15 we leave for a short drive. We go past haying machines, an irrigated melon field, and an orchard of crabapples, all large consumers of precious water. I've been told that this has been a drought year, as have most previous years since the early 1980s. Precipitation is currently less than normal, temperatures are higher, and dust storms are more frequent. Mongolia is an arid and windy country with many sunny days, and rainwater evaporates quickly without percolating into the soil. Groundwater tends to be saline. This Gobi desert region receives only 2 to 4 inches (50–100 mm) of precipitation a year. The adjoining steppe to the north averages about 6 to 10 inches, and Ulaan Bataar, near the edge of the northern forests, about 15 inches. Over 80 percent of the country is rangeland, susceptible to desertification, and only 2.5 percent is considered suitable for agriculture, all features indicative of the country's ecological constraints.

I wonder if the use of so much precious water by Bayan Tooroi from the nearby hills will have an impact on the level of groundwater upon which the park oases depend and that the wildlife needs to survive. There is already a drop in water table, I've been told, and critical springs have dried up. Large stands of the woody shrub saxaul, *Haloxylon ammodendron,* have died in the drought. These gnarled shrubs, five feet (1.5 m) or more tall, stand now leafless, depriving camels of one of their principal foods. *Gobi,* after all, comes from the Chinese *gebi,* signifying either "a waterless place" or "stony ground." I absorb this information without much comment—at present.

We stop at a ger. A smiling woman greets us, wearing a traditional ankle-length *deel* or *del* (gown) of sparkling blue and a green cap. She cuddles a young saiga antelope, a charming gray-brown animal with a large, bulbous muzzle and gentle eyes. Three small saiga populations persist in Mongolia. The government wants to establish another one here, a desolate place where these animals have not been known

A herder woman cuddles a young saiga antelope, which she is raising.

to exist before. A total of 104 young were captured and fostered by domestic goats between 1985 and 1989. Those that survived have been released, and these now number 38.

The short, pale-white horns of the saiga are much in demand in Chinese traditional medicine. Almost as valuable as rhino horn or the musk of musk deer, saiga horn medicine, called *lin yan jiao* by the Chinese, is said to cure high fever, convulsions, hypertension, and other ailments. Tens of thousands of saiga antelope have been killed, legally and illegally, in Kazakhstan and elsewhere in Central Asia in recent years. Whether the species will survive in Mongolia is uncertain.

In a corral are four wild camels, two years old or older, together with several domestic camels. Domestic and wild camels readily hybridize, even though their DNA show enough difference to classify them as separate subspecies. Local herders encourage such hybridization to produce fast racing camels. The government allows herders with their livestock to penetrate the buffer zone of the park in times of drought, as at present, and herds of the two kinds of camel readily mix. Park authorities have already shot several hybrids in the park in an attempt to keep the rare wild strain pure. Why, then, are these two forms of camel allowed to live together? Why are domestic and wild camels permitted to compete for the same sparse forage in the park? Is the system based on a plan, on indifference, or on carelessness? I hesitate to ask because it would be an implied criticism. And I am new to a country in which until recently "bourgeois elements" were purged. Afterward I regret my caution. As I wrote in my 1998 *Wildlife of the Tibetan Steppe:*

> Between 1987 and 1991, a total of 22 camel young (10 males, 12 females) were captured in the Great Gobi National Park ostensibly for captive breeding. Nine of the young soon died, but the rest (6 males, 7 females) were raised by free-ranging domestic camel females around Bayan Tooroi, the park headquarters. When these young camels matured, the park authorities failed to segregate the wild and domestic animals. One female, born in 1987, was bred by a domestic male and gave birth to a hybrid in 1992 and a second hybrid in 1994.

The rarity of the wild camels makes them of special concern, and they should not be casually hybridized. The camels are critically endangered and so listed by international conventions such as the World Conservation Union (IUCN) and Convention on International Trade in Endangered Species (CITES). Mongolia and China have also given these animals full legal protection.

Observing the wild and domestic camels together enables us to see the differences between them more clearly. The domestic camels

We ask directions from a herder leading his large-humped domestic camel in the Gobi desert.

are bulkier, woolier, and darker in color. Their humps are large and misshapen, and they have much hair on the crown. The wild ones, by contrast, are slim and lean, with a light gray-brown coat and small, tidy conical humps. A plow horse compared to a race horse.

Tulgat tells me, with Chuka translating, that there are about five hundred wild camels in the park but that they are probably decreasing in number. They mate from December to February and give birth in March and April after a gestation period of about four hundred days. Thus, if the young survives, a female will give birth only once every two years. They reach sexual maturity at four to five years. Tulgat will perhaps show me his camel census figures. I discern the emphasis on the word *perhaps*. I had already been told that Mongolian scientists are reluctant to share data with foreigners because, to quote one, "The Russians come here and steal our data. And we do not see it again."

Two rare and endangered species, the saiga and camel, are being "managed" without much concern for their potential hybridization or decline here at Bayan Tooroi. I need to escape being confronted with such problems by heading into the wild, at least for a while. Rising alone out of the desert on the far horizon is the Holy Mother Mountain, a massive slab of eroded granite. The track to the mountain crosses crusted and buckled saline soil. The landscape is one of austere and glaring emptiness. At one site is a mound with a spring bubbling out of the ground. It is traditional to stop to take a drink of the fresh cold water. Four goitered or black-tailed gazelle flee at the sight of our car. We climb the barren mountain, the rocks vibrating in the heat, watched by yellowish *Agama* lizards with red and green freckles. The exercise revives me. The rocky slopes glow softly in the setting sun as we retrace our steps down the mountain. Back at Bayan Tooroi we have *buus* for dinner, a favorite local dish of deep-fried mutton dumplings. As we eat, the television blasts raucous American rock music with a British accent, a Russian program from Poland beamed to Mongolia.

We leave in two jeeps and a truck, heading southeast toward an oasis over 50 miles (80 km) away.

The terrain is flat rising to hilly, stony and wind blasted, a desiccated landscape with a scatter of low shrubs. The truck stalls. While the drivers try to fix some faulty wiring, we wander nearby. Thin sprouts of wild onion and a rare low shrub of the genus *Iljinia* with fleshy leaves are the only green. Tulgat notes that wild camels like the leaves of that shrub. I find them juicy but sour. The truck fixed, we continue. The truck stalls again and again, while we wait among ruins of rock or on scorching sands. When the sun is only a glowing red orb teetering on the horizon, our jeeps race ahead toward the campsite, leaving the truck to follow. The camp consists of a lone pump house and a livestock trough among black-stoned hills. Our only wildlife sighting today was the four black-tailed gazelles fleeing frantically. The truck arrives around midnight and within two hours continues toward our destination, the Shar Khuls oasis, while the rest of us sleep.

The next day our route winds through a maze of brittle dark rocks among naked hills through a large valley and then down into a vast depression. A few shrubs with green leafless stems draw my focus on the gravel plain. Another camel food, I'm told, of the genus *Ephedra*. Ahead is a jagged range, and at the mouth of a valley is a stand of cottonwood, a seeming mirage in these badlands. Tamarisk (*Tamarix*) shrubs are there too, five feet high and heathlike, with scaly leaves. An expanse of tall *Phragmites* reed almost fills the valley floor for several hundred feet, a good sign of water. Both the shrubs and reeds provide food for camels as well. The truck is already at our campsite, set up rather too close to the only water source for wildlife in the area. We join the others there.

Tulgat, Chuka, and I then explore the oasis. We find several small pools, the water clear, cold, and somewhat salty. Near one of them is a large metal dispenser of the kind that provides nutritious food pellets to livestock. But this one is for Gobi bears, one of about a dozen such dispensers scattered around the park. Looking at the stark terrain of the Gobi, I can well imagine that the bears benefit from food supplements, especially in times of drought, as at present. The bears obviously like these livestock pellets, for their mushy feces litter the site. I look around alertly. Could a bear be hiding in the reeds? The Gobi bears are said to be fairly small, adults weighing just 125 to 300 pounds (57–136 kg). But a startled and disgruntled bear weighing even that little … One must interact with animals on their own terms, and I do not know these bears yet.

We find the paw print of a wolf and the pad prints of a wild camel in the mud. I measure the latter, which are 8 inches (20 cm) long, a trivial fact but of the kind upon which I can build a framework of the local ecology. There is pleasure in what we observe around this oasis, but an even greater pleasure comes from the visions our observations generate of camels and bears and all the other species which gather here as if at a sacred site, dependent on the water of life. As the poet William Blake wrote in *The Marriage of Heaven and Hell* (1773): "For everything that lives is holy, life delights in life."

Tulgat suggests that we hide on a ridge overlooking the oasis. Sometimes argali sheep come here to drink. The argali is the largest of all *Ovis* sheep, and the males sport massive, curled horns. The argali are slimmer than the stocky wild sheep that, for example, occur in North America and live near cliffs to which they escape in times of danger, and they have lithe, long legs. They are adapted to escape predators by fleeing across open terrain. I had observed argali on the Tibetan Plateau, where they are now rare, but those are considered a separate subspecies. After we have waited an hour, a female argali appears, trailed by a large young. They have gray-brown coats, a white rump patch, and a white-tipped muzzle. The eddying wind apparently sends them our scent, for they veer away without drinking at the pool.

After waiting a while longer, we drive west a few miles with only one jeep to check on a small oasis. The driver, whose name is given only as Enkhbat, like so many Mongolians drives vehicles the way he would ride horses: flat out. I ask him to slow down. Kay and I already have throbbing backaches from the headlong drives. Two wild camels startle ahead of us, the first I've seen. Our Mongolian colleagues want to give chase. My *no* is emphatic. Why frighten the animals to no purpose? Extend to them a feeling of kinship and show their hard lives some compassion. The two camels had been heading toward the oasis, which consisted of only muddy seepages. Now they move off across the desert and soon dissolve in the heat haze. Camels, I have read, can go for a week without water and then will drink several gallons at one time. On the way back to camp we spot a lone Mongolian wild ass, or khulan, pale as the sand in the distance.

Sustained, intimate wildlife observations here will, I realize, certainly take perseverance and depend on luck.

Our next goal the following day, August 25, is the Tsagaan Burgas Bulak oasis to the east. Tulgat says, "Khavtgai," and points ahead. Far out on the plain are eight camels walking single file in stately procession, an image of power and grace. They have not yet seen us. They are heading toward the oasis just beyond a low ridge. Tulgat indicates that we should wait here for a while. We sit in the car for two hours, and then walk silently ahead on foot. Kay prefers to wait for our return. We walk through a maze of ravines and over low ridges until we reach a crest with a view of the oasis. It is 2:00 p.m. The camels are there, seven of them lying down and one standing. They face in all directions, as if alert for any danger. The wind is in the wrong direction to mask our scent, but it suddenly shifts in our favor. Tulgat motions me to come, and the two of us sneak to another knoll closer to the animals. I am entranced and filled with joy. Finally I can watch undisturbed camels leading their desert life. This is what I have come for: not just information on food habits and group size but the intimate details of their being. Even so, I recognize that I can observe their behavior but not really understand them. It's even difficult for me to understand another human being, including Kay after three decades of marriage.

The camels become restless at four. One female rolls onto her side several times, taking a dust bath. Two lurch up onto their feet, hind legs first and then with a lunge upward onto the front legs. Congenially the two rub rumps. I wonder if they have an itch. They are still shedding the last of their winter wool. Then, as if on signal, one I fail to detect, all amble through a willow thicket and tall reeds toward water about 650 feet (200 m) away. Tulgat and I cross the valley and hide near the waterhole. Most camels are out of sight. I hear them yip and grunt; one trumpets like an elephant. They reappear, grazing on reeds and browsing on willows. They return to the water, then spread out to feed some more, one reaching for cottonwood leaves. At eight, after six hours of observation and with the evening light mellow on the rumpled hills, we leave quietly. Kay has awaited our return patiently. When we check the waterhole at a later date, we find a shallow pool, small enough to step across, smelling of sulfur. Near it are five Gobi bear droppings wholly composed of purple berries from the *Nitraria* shrubs which grow around oases.

Another day, another oasis. It is Kay's and my wedding anniversary, our thirty-second. I note a rifle in the car and ask its purpose. To shoot wolves is the reply. Wolves have no protection in Mongolia and can be killed at will. I once more respond with an emphatic *no*. I do not want to be directly associated with any killings. We should respect the lives of other species, especially in a national park. Chuka has already explained to me that wolves are too abundant in the park and that they kill too many young camels. To save the camels, wolf numbers need to be controlled. A total of 37 wolves were shot in 1987 and 38 in 1988. So far 29 wolves have been killed this year, 8 adults and 21 young, the last-named taken as pups from dens. I would be shown the research data on our return and would be able to make up my own mind. I remember with disgust the uncontrolled and unjustified wolf slaughter by the Alaska Department of Fish and Game in northern Alaska while I was a student at the university there in the early 1950s. Over 30,000 wolves had already been killed in the 1980s in Mongolia's wolf extermination campaign because wolves are "a malicious enemy of domestic animals," according to one government statement. There is a Mongolian saying: "Man without luck can't meet wolf; man with luck can meet wolf; man with more luck than wolf can shoot it." For several years after this trip, during the 1990s, the wolf hunts in the Gobi almost ceased because park rangers could not get gasoline for their motorcycles after the collapse of the economy.

For now, we drive into the canyon of a rocky range and then continue on foot. At the base of a cliff is a scrape made by a snow leopard, the animal having raked its hind paws in the sand to leave a sign of its presence. Snow leopard! I know that these cats are supposed to be here, but I'm still startled. After all, I'm used to finding their spoor in the alpine zone at ten thousand feet and higher in the Himalayas and other ranges, not in baking-hot desert. The Gobi is teaching me the adaptability of animals. I then find a soft, fresh bear dropping. I poke my finger into it to judge its temperature and determine whether we might meet the bear around the next bend. The dropping is cool, deposited last night. A dispenser of livestock pellets is located on the other side of a low ridge. We wait near it for two hours hoping to see a bear. Only a cackling flock of fifteen chukar partridges wanders by. We have seen little wildlife today. On our return to camp, Kay informs us that three argali, one a large male, had come to water. Our dinner is at ten and Spartan as usual: a bowl of mutton soup and bread. Amarzhargal, one team member, is conspicuously withdrawn and not enjoying himself the way the others are. Perhaps he has been ordered to come on the expedition to monitor us. Once he had stated plaintively, "I'm not interested in conservation." He had majored in Spanish literature at a university in Odessa, Ukraine.

We move again, this time westward to the Bogt Tsagaan Ders oasis. It consists of a small patch of green by an outwash plain near a series of hills extending north to the rugged Atas Bogd Range. We walk cautiously to a hillock overlooking the oasis. Sixteen camels are at the edge of the oasis crowded together, neither grazing nor drinking, just standing or lying down. There is not a single young among these camels. Four khulan are there too, three grazing and one taking a dust bath. These four then leave. Suddenly the camels flee in a tight bunch. I think they might have scented us. But then two wolves howl and trot into view on a ridge crest. The camels move in single file off across the plain. A while later we check the waterholes: there are several seepages, none more than an inch or two (2.5–5 cm) deep.

Two herds, one of nine and one of twelve camels, approach the oasis the following day, probably some of the animals we had seen earlier. The wind eddies, and both herds stop abruptly, as if they had slammed into a wall. They cluster, mill around, and move away, to my consternation. I feel mortified that we have prevented them from drinking and forced them to make a long trek to water elsewhere. Their shyness around people and cars, which the camels no doubt have encountered fairly commonly, suggests only one thing to me: they have been hunted for meat.

Seven miles (11 km) to the south is another small oasis at the base of a hill near a dry riverbed. Once again Tulgat, Chuka, and I sneak closer. Two khulan males stand on top of hillocks advertising themselves, showing off their sleek power to all the other wild asses in the vicinity. But it is hot, and they stand with heads lowered. One sees me trying to photograph and reluctantly leaves. Farther away are three more. I presume that khulan are territorial, the males defending a piece of turf and waiting for wandering females. Khulan are handsome in their light tan-and-white coats with short black manes, a dark line along the backbone, and a long, black tail tassel. But they tend to blend so well into the landscape that the males need to make themselves conspicuous on hilltops.

Ten camels are at the oasis in the tall reeds and tamarisk bushes,

Wild Bactrian camels and wild asses (khulan)
visit a water hole in the Gobi desert.

four at the water. They drink only briefly as if there were little water. After a drink a camel shakes its head up and down, lips flopping and water spraying. And then they squabble. One camel will rear its head and neck back and open its mouth with growls and yips. Its tail will beat, eel-like, back and forth. With their small heads and long necks they look reptilian, successors to the dinosaurs whose ancient remains litter some parts of the Gobi. Now about a dozen khulan arrive, and some move to within 10 to 15 feet of the camels near the water. But the camels are possessive. If a khulan crowds near, the camel steps closer, muzzle raised high, towering above, threatening until the other retreats. When the camels vacate the waterhole, the khulan move in. However, one female camel has tarried, and in her sedate way she drives the khulan back repeatedly by simply walking toward them.

An argali female suddenly shows up at the oasis and mingles with the camels and khulan. She shies aside when a khulan approaches her.

To have three rare wildlife species congregate at this oasis is to me a special Gobi gift that reveals the spirit of the land. The camels disperse. A khulan stallion emits a wheezing bray and chases others with muzzle raised and tail arched. At 5:40 p.m. all the animals have left, and we too depart, after six hours of observations.

For two more days we check oases. It rained heavily one night, a downpour that offered new life to all desert beings. Wild animals now have no need to visit waterholes. We tally a few more black-tailed gazelles and measure an old argali skull, a male six and a half years old, judging by the age rings on the horns. We return to Bayan Tooroi on September 3, having driven 523 miles (837 km).

We stay in Bayan Tooroi for a day to share and review our data, especially the camel data. Our count is 106 camels, a few perhaps seen more than once. Yet there is not a single young camel among them. Zero. Such young should now be about five months old. Tulgat's annual park censuses show that in the seven years from 1982 to 1988 the average percentage of camel young in the population was only 4.8 with a range of 2.5 to 9.3 percent. The figure for 1989 is, I later find out, 3.1 percent. (In 1997 it was 4.2, in 1998 it was 5.5, and in 1999 it was 7.3, to give some later figures that were communicated to me.) A comparison of counts made right after the birth season and later in the year shows a decline in the number of young. In 1987, for example, there were 13.8 percent young in the population in April and only 2.5 percent in October. What happens to the youngsters? Of 89 camels found dead over five years in the latter part of the 1980s, 54 (61 percent) had apparently been killed by wolves, most of these young animals, and two by snow leopards. However, it is sometimes unclear if a predator has actually killed the animal or is scavenging on one already dead.

Fights between rutting males also cause an occasional death. During the rut, which begins in November, adult males aged eight to ten years or more try to gather a harem of a dozen or more females, which they then vigorously defend against other males. One male may attempt to intimidate another by flicking urine with his tail, rubbing the musk gland located on the back of his head against his hump, and grinding his teeth. But if this does not work, he might slash the other with his large canines. As Sven Hedin observed in *Central Asia and Tibet* (1903): "They mangle one another terribly with their teeth, and very often tear large pieces of flesh out of one another." Poachers also kill camels for their meat on occasion. I'm told that camels that leave the park and drift across the border into China are particularly vulnerable to poachers.

Wolves obviously have an important impact on the camel population. With oases few and widely scattered, wolves have merely to wait at a water source for wildlife to appear sooner or later, especially in drought years, as now. We observed an instance of that. Interestingly, camel mothers apparently do not defend their young against wolves, but khulan mothers are said to do so. Perhaps that is why 11.5 percent of the khulan we saw had foals at heel. As Tulgat and I noted in a joint 1992 scientific paper in the journal *Biological Conservation*, "Status and Distribution of Wild Bactrian Camels": "Of five wolf stomachs examined in 1987–89 all contained the remains of camel young."

A still unanswered question concerns the percentage of adult females that perhaps fail to give birth. Some camels at the oases were in poor physical condition: thin, with ribs clearly outlined beneath a slack hide. Forage is seasonally sparse, dry, and low in nutrients, especially during the prolonged current drought. Oases are decreasing in number, and camels have to travel far in the heat to reach them. Females might simply not conceive or might abort a pregnancy under such harsh conditions, another factor that may help explain the low percentage of young.

Survival of camel young is so poor during many years that it will inevitably lead to a declining population. The camel population would need to average around 10 percent young at year's end to endure, not the current 5 percent. After receiving these data from Tulgat, I tended to agree with the park authorities that occasional wolf control is desirable to maintain this critically endangered species in the park, among the last of their kind. Yet this conclusion is for me a moral and ethical balancing act. I intensely dislike the idea of killing wolves and doubt that there is at this point enough solid information about the long-term impact of these wolves on the camel population to justify a hunt. Still, the survival of the wild camels is an imperative. Where is the ecological equilibrium between wolves and camels?

Several fragmented small camel populations persist in China, as I noted in wide-ranging surveys of the Xinjiang region between 1985 and 1988. One such population survives along the Tarim River in the Taklimakan Desert. Other populations extend from the northern edge of the Tibet Plateau, from the Arjin Mountains north into the great Gashun Gobi desert, with the dry lakebed of Lop Nur at its center. There Nikolay Przhevalsky (Przewalski) recorded the wild camel first in 1877. He describes the situation in his 1879 book *From Kulja, Across the Tian Shan to Lob-Nor:*

Twenty years ago, wild camels were numerous near Lake Lob [Lop Nur], where the village of Chargalik now stands, and farther to the east along the foot of the Altyn-tagh, as well as in the range itself. Our guide, a hunter of Chargalik, told us that it was not unusual in those days, to see some dozens, or even a hundred of these animals together.... With an increase of population at Chargalik, the hunters of Lob-nor became more numerous, and the camels scarcer.... Years may pass without so much as one being seen; in more favourable seasons again the native hunters kill their five and six during the summer and autumn.

Expeditions such as this, and later ones by Sven Hedin and others, further decimated the camels, which they shot for food.

It is worth noting that the last wild one-humped camel of North Africa became extinct about two thousand years ago, though domestic camels persist. The Bactrian camel may have been first domesticated as recently as five to six thousand years ago in northwestern China. By the eleventh century CE, detailed ancient texts had been written that described efficient methods of Bactrian camel husbandry; one even contained a list of forty-eight camel diseases.

I am interested in taking a quick look at Gobi B, the Strictly Protected Area west of here, even though wild camels and Gobi bears do not occur there. Park director Chuluun, age sixty-two, accompanies us. On the way he informs us that he grew up in this area. Fifty years ago, Mongolian gazelles and Przewalski's horses, first described by Nikolai Przewalski in 1878, could still be found here, but both species were shot out, the last-named exterminated throughout the whole country. But the horse's tale has a good ending. The Przewalski's horse is a large-headed, stocky, dun horse with an erect black mane and long tail hairs. The Mongolians call it *takhi,* "spirit" or "worthy of worship." Hearing of this unique wild horse, in 1899 Friedrich Falz-Fein caught and imported a number of the horses to his estate in Ukraine, where they thrived. Many zoos and institutions then bred this rare horse until there were over a thousand in captivity. After our visit, a major move to return the takhi to its homeland was instigated by the Swiss biologist Claudia Feh in the 1990s. Fourteen horses were brought from Holland in May 1992 to a special reserve, Khustai Nuruu, near Ulaan Bataar, where I visited them that year.

There they have bred well. The Khustai Nuruu reserve was upgraded to national park in 1998. Other free-living horse herds are now also in China and Kazakhstan. But now, as we head west toward Gobi B, Chuluun notes with contentment that the takhi will soon be reintroduced back here to his old home area. It did indeed happen, in 2003.

We drive around the Gobi B Strictly Protected Area for three days, checking oases and scanning the desert expanses with their thin shrub cover for wildlife. We tally 147 black-tailed gazelles and 107 khulan. What startles me is the extreme fright of these animals on detecting a vehicle. I'm told in confidence that about 400 khulan were officially shot the previous year for meat. I am beginning to wonder if Mongolia looks at its wild treasures simply as natural resources to be plundered no matter where, even in Strictly Protected Areas such as this.

I am ready to leave. My mind is on the future, on perhaps studying snow leopards, Gobi bears, and Mongolian gazelles. These species have been specifically mentioned to me as of interest to the Ministry of Nature and Environment. I would like to set up these projects but not to remain here for years to study each species in detail. That would be the responsibility of Mongolian biologists. Would I find dedicated fieldworkers here? I also muse about the coming effects of the "openness" policy when the Russians pull out of the country. Will the country become more unstable? Mongolians have a historical reputation for unruliness. Already there are food and gasoline shortages. Would I be able to conduct the research?

After leaving the park, we cross a rocky range and descend onto a plain, the Shargyn Gobi. Several saiga antelope flee from the car in a characteristic posture with head and neck lowered, looking like fawn-colored, scurrying rodents. There are about seven hundred saiga antelope in this area, according to Chuka. Joel Berger and his team radio-collared several of these saiga, as described in his book *Extreme Conservation,* and found that they ranged over an area of up to 1,800 square miles (4,662 km²).

We return to the provincial town of Altai in a hailstorm. There we have an interview with Mr. Agyajav, the vice chairman of the executive committee of Gobi-Altai *aimak,* or province. We provide him with our wildlife information and impressions, and he offers us useful statistics about the province. It is 55,440 square miles (143,590 km²) in size with a human population of sixty thousand, half of whom are sixteen years old or under. There are about two million head of livestock, two-thirds of them sheep.

Back in Ulaan Bataar (UB) we have discussions about my returning later this year for a preliminary snow leopard survey. I worry about protection for the cat. Mongolia has, after China, more snow leopards than any of the twelve other countries in which the species occurs. In 1987, Mongolia opened up trophy hunting of snow leopards by foreigners. A safari company, Kleinburger Brothers, charged ten thousand dollars to arrange a hunt and the Mongolian government demanded fourteen thousand dollars for a license. Five of the cats were shot before the international outcry against such commercialism of a rare species prodded the government to rescind the program. One argument for a trophy hunt was that snow leopards killed an inordinate amount of livestock, but it turned out that county officials had greatly exaggerated their figures to receive more compensation from the government. Yet in July of that year, a Mongol Press bulletin noted that an Austrian hunter named Keindel had come with two dogs and killed a snow leopard in the Gobi desert. "Thousands of foreign tourists come to Mongolia every year to see the beautiful Gobi and to hunt," the bulletin noted. "A marvelous skin and the excitement of chasing became excellent compensation for all the efforts and expenses." The concept of conservation had obviously not as yet been absorbed by the local media.

Many countries, including the United States, prohibit the importation of certain endangered species, including trophies obtained legally elsewhere. At least one snow leopard skin from Mongolia was smuggled into the United States in the late 1980s. With marvelous persistence the Department of Law Enforcement of the Fish and Wildlife Service pursued the matter until the culprit was caught in 1994 and fined ten thousand dollars. For a while, Mongolia banned such trophy hunting. In 2000, a revised hunting law prohibited the sale or purchase of snow leopards or any of their parts. Yet in 2011 Mongolia tried to open up trophy hunting for snow leopards again. This time it was billed as "for scientific purposes." After another international outcry the government revoked its decision within three weeks.

I have never seen a Mongolian gazelle in its habitat. Before deciding whether to make a future study of the species, Kay and I want to obtain impressions of the animals in their habitat, the *menengiin,* the endless eastern steppe. On September 15, 1989, Tserendeleg, Chuka, Kay, and I fly to the city of Choibalsan in Dornod Province at the edge of the steppe. It is Mongolia's fourth-largest city, with a population of about forty thousand. The city is named for Khorloogiin Choibalsan, head of the People's Revolutionary Party and ultimately a dictator and an instigator of the Great Terror from the late 1920s until his death in 1952.

With unwavering loyalty to Joseph Stalin and the Soviet Union, Choibalsan was determined to liquidate in purges all "foreign interventionist forces and internal class enemies" and all "bourgeois elements" as he relentlessly encouraged "leftist socialist reforms." This included the execution of over one thousand heads of household, especially those of the feudal nobility, and confiscation of their land

and livestock. To achieve and retain power he executed many top party and military officials as well as thirty-six of fifty-one members of the country's Central Committee.

Mongolia's Buddhist church had in the 1920s nearly as large an annual income as the government. The many monasteries, with their large landholdings, were powerful and had considerable public support; it was traditional for a family to give one son to the church. As a result around 35 percent of the country's adult male population lived in monasteries, and the monks operated as a conservative force against the socialist designs of the ruling party, resisting changes. How better to wrench economic and political control from the monasteries than by simply destroying Lamaism in the country? In the late 1930s at least seventeen thousand "counterrevolutionary monks" were executed, thousands more were imprisoned, and most of the rest were forced back into civilian life. A total of 746 monasteries were demolished, religious objects were smashed, and texts were burned. As Jasper Becker notes in *The Lost Country,* during Choibalsan's rule "Around 100,000 innocent people were executed," and many of the deaths took place "during the purges of the late 1930s." Such purges affected all levels of society, as stated by Owen Lattimore in *Nomads and Commissars* (1962): "Following the expropriation of 669 noble families in 1929, the property of another 837 households was expropriated in 1930–31, including the property of 205 high ecclesiastical figures. And this time, ominously, 711 heads of households were put to death or imprisoned, on the accusation of having opposed the power of the state." Mongolia was emulating Stalin's Great Terror of 1937 and 1938, when at its height about fifteen hundred citizens were executed every day. Most top military and government officials were killed by Stalin, and several million others died in prison camps and by starvation. No one knows how many persons actually were liquidated by Choibalsan, and today there is great reluctance in the country to discuss and write about this recent history, this harvest of sorrow and descent into moral darkness.

The town of Choibalsan retains its name.

The years of terror almost destroyed the cultural and environmental cohesion and ethical values of the country that had developed over the centuries, as described so well in *The Mongolian Landscape Tradition* by Pieter Germeraad and Zandangin Enebisch. "The feudal nobility and Lamaistic clergy can be considered the main actors in the traditional land use and environmental conservation policy, since they issued and controlled the rights for the use of the land. In the feudal Mongolian nomadic communities there existed a unity of knowledge regarding the correct use of the land transmitted via for example religious manuscripts and orally transmitted stories and legends. Social behavior, which caused within the community a unity of social relations and individual obligations towards each other and the surrounding environment, played in this a major role."

Adding to this internal turmoil at that time was Japan's invasion of Manchuria in northeast China in July 1937, its occupation of parts of Inner Mongolia in 1938, and its threat to annex Mongolia. Several major battles took place between Japan and the Russian and Mongolian military until the end of World War II in 1945.

After Choibalsan's death, Yumjaagiin Tsendenbal continued totalitarian rule for forty-four years until he was removed in 1984, when he was spending more time in Russia than tending to business in Mongolia. The economy stagnated, and there were occasional riots. Choibalsan had initiated an effort toward collective ownership of all property. Tsendenbal, in contrast, wanted "to exterminate the concept of property." Nearly all livestock was still in private hands in 1947, but all herders had by 1959 been forced to belong to a cooperative, a *negdel.* These cooperatives were highly unpopular. Many landowners slaughtered their livestock, gave up rural life, and moved into towns. To placate the negdels, the government then allowed each household to own a limited amount of livestock, depending on number of family members. For example, a family of six could have forty-two sheep or sixty goats or six cattle.

Now, in 1989, I hope that Mongolia, after these decades of turbulence, is on a rapid road to recovery. Certainly I'm deeply grateful to the country and my colleagues for treating me, a naturalist from America, so hospitably. Everyone here continues to live in the recent past, with its restrictive laws, its purges, and the vague spiritual influence of Buddhism. When on occasion I ask a historical question out of curiosity, the answer tends to be skirted or the truth reorganized, and any problems are blamed on the Russians. There has been much that is positive, it is rightly stressed: in education, schooling for children between the ages of six and fourteen is compulsory and 96 percent of the population is literate; health care is free; and transportation is improved. The country's good fortune comes from simultaneously moving toward something and moving away from something.

N. Ganbaatar, of a local conservation society and hunting organization, has met us on arrival in Choibalsan. Rugged and energetic, he tells us about his work with *dzeren,* the Mongolian gazelle. He estimates that at least three hundred thousand remain on the steppe, making this the largest concentration of any ungulate species in Asia today. Yet many thousands are shot annually by government teams in late November and December, a total of over two hundred thousand during the 1980s. The frozen carcasses are sold to Sweden, Holland, Yugoslavia, Germany, and other countries whose population like to eat wildlife meat.

*Commercial government hunts once killed thousands
of Mongolian gazelles for export.*

Ganbaatar is guiding us on a four-day tour of the steppe. West of Choibalsan, among low hills, is an eruption of a tan-colored *Microtus* vole. Dozens scurry back and forth across the road. Attracted by these abundant rodents, many upland hawks have congregated; one is perched on almost every telephone pole. An occasional steppe eagle circles overhead. A Corsac fox bounds along the track ahead of us, gray and tan, with a bushy white-tipped tail. The terrain becomes flatter, the endless steppe. We see only grass and more grass to the horizon. As the Russian poet Alexander Pushkin said, "That wondrous vastness delights my eyes." A herd of about 350 Mongolian gazelles flees, too far away for me to count. After driving 80 miles (130 km) we see our first ger and some livestock. Farther on, after nearly 200 miles of bumpy tracks, we reach a tourist camp of several gers by a lake, Buyr Nuur, on the border of China. Part of today's route was along the border demarcated by a skimpy fence of barbed wire.

Low dark clouds hang over the steppe the next day, and a raw wind thrashes the grassland. I walk briefly along the lake's edge and record a northern lapwing and a white saker falcon. Not even the hamster-like pikas, usually so visible and abundant, leave their snug burrows in such weather. Kay and I burrow into our ger with cups of hot tea.

Continuing on toward the county town of Matad, we come across about a thousand Mongolian gazelles spread across the steppe. I grab my spotting scope and try to melt into a patch of grass, focusing on a herd moving in a long line as I try to classify each animal. The result: 42 adult males, 13 yearling males just over a year old, 157 females, and 68 young, a total of 280. It is sheer pleasure to watch these lovely gazelle in their sparkling tawny coats with the white heart-shaped rump patch. The males have short, curved, bumpy horns, about a foot long, that flare outward and slightly inward at the tips. The throat of adult males is conspicuously enlarged, almost like a goiter, on the lower neck. Yes, I definitely must return and learn more about the life of these gazelles. Roy Chapman Andrews wrote in *Ends of the Earth,* in 1929: "Never again will I have such feelings as Mongolia gave me. The broad sweeps of dun gravel merging into a vague horizon, the ancient trails once traveled by Genghis Khan's wild raiders.... All these thrilled me to the core." This endless steppe, this fleeting glimpse into the past, evokes in me a similar response.

We return to Choibalsan the next day, completing a brief survey of 583 miles (933 km), and ready to return to UB. Boarding the flight in Choibalsan turns out to be a casual and disorderly affair. No ticket is checked, and we load our own gear into the baggage hold. People come onto the plane to bid farewell to family and friends and then depart. An old woman stands by the plane with a bowl of milk and uses a spoon to flick the milk against the plane, thereby wishing our journey good luck.

This account, based on my 1989 visit, at a time when the country was just emerging from decades of historical turmoil, is designed to illustrate my first steps when establishing a project in a country new to me, one in which I don't speak the language. I have to contact all relevant institutions and seek their assistance, including the U.S. embassy. I must learn what actions will be possible, and meet officials, potential colleagues, and local people, all in the context of the country's history, scientific needs, and conservation plans. I must find out how best to help the country. The people and I need to learn to understand each other and establish a measure of trust. This requires meetings, congenial field trips, shared information, and donation of needed equipment, and it inevitably also means uncertainty and lost days. But it also leads to mutual satisfaction.

On this first visit, Dembereldorj and Tserendeleg take Kay and me on a special outing just before we leave Mongolia. Adjoining UB is a mountain range covered with birch and larch, the leaves now in autumn gold. It is the holy Bogd Khan Uul, one of the oldest wildlife reserves in the world, established in 1758. Monks once patrolled and protected it. In the late 1920s, several Russians sneaked into the holy reserve and killed a bear. A furious mob of monks captured the Russians and brought them back in chains. The guardian spirit of these mountains, as well as of UB, is the Khangarid, an eagle-like bird similar to the Garuda of Hindu mythology. The spirit is a symbol of courage and honesty.

Our interest in the reserve is benign. The slopes of the Bogd Uul are the home of red deer, or maral. We soon encounter a herd of sixty-one maral in a valley, mostly does and fawns but also one large-antlered stag. Dark clouds settle over the valley. The white rump patches of the deer shine in the somber light. Nearby is a herd of

A red deer stag bugles during the rut in the hills near Ulaan Baatar.

about thirty maral, again with one large stag. He follows a doe and sniffs her rump, whereupon she urinates and he sniffs that too, testing to see whether she is in heat. He raises his muzzle and bugles, a sonorous, haunting sound. The rut has begun.

Having sampled various species and habitats during this visit, I must now take the next steps for the future. We sign an agreement to continue our collaboration on snow leopards, Gobi bears, and Mongolian gazelles. I feel somewhat guilty for abandoning the camels as a focus of study, especially after they provided me with such delightful observations. But I would return to their Gobi habitat and keep an eye on them to see if my recommendations to the ministry are being considered. These suggestions include making accurate counts of population size using standardized techniques and detailed long-term monitoring of the animals to determine birth rates and survival of young, causes of death, and other aspects affecting the herds. Domestic livestock should be banned from the park, especially during droughts, when wild and domestic camels compete more fiercely for scarce forage: there is not enough for both. Laws and regulations must be strictly enforced to prevent poaching, mining, and other illegal activities. No one should be allowed to camp within a certain distance of an oasis, denying wildlife access to water. With oases drying up, new water sources should, if possible, be made. Camels and other wildlife from the park travel across the border into China, and closer cooperation between the two countries is essential. Detailed yearlong studies of the ecology of the rangelands are needed, as well as of various species, including wolves, Gobi bears, khulan, and black-tailed gazelles. Education of local communities and their direct involvement in conservation of the park is essential. A major effort should be made to enhance household livelihoods, something that tourism could help promote. Finally, purposeful or negligent hybridization of wild and domestic camels should be banned, and punished if it occurs.

The flight to Beijing has only about a dozen passengers, one a chunky, middle-aged American hunter. He proclaims across the aisle to Kay and me that he had paid thirty thousand dollars to shoot an argali sheep in the Altai Mountains. "The largest on record," he says. He shot it on the first day in the field and left immediately, happy to rush back to Chicago. Where precisely has he been? He has no idea. I take away from Mongolia a far greater treasure in my notes, memories, and feelings.

Three decades have passed since that first encounter with the wild camels in 1989. But I have sought news about the camels through personal contact with Mongolian and Western colleagues and by perusing the literature. Especially useful to me has been a volume titled *Ecology and Conservation of Wild Bactrian Camels* (Camelus bactrianus ferus), edited by Richard Reading, Dulamtserengiin Enkhbileg, and Tuvdendorjiin Galbaatar, and published in 2002 by the Mongolian Conservation Coalition. It is to me a great satisfaction to note in the report that many Mongolians and Chinese and a few Westerners have devoted time and effort to gather information that will help the protection and management of the wild camels. A main goal has been to count them. In Gobi A, such counts are usually made by driving along transect lines and recording all camels within a certain distance. The results, based on statistics and intuition, tend to be approximate, and numbers have generally ranged from 400 to 800 camels in counts during the 1970s and 1980s within the 12,820 square miles (33,200 km²) of camel range. In more recent years the counts tended to vary from 300 to 500 camels, with most in the range of 400 to 500. An exception is an aerial survey, the results published in a 1999 issue of the journal *Oryx* by Richard Reading and his coworkers. They presented the startling number of 1,985 camels, plus or minus 802, based on statistical modeling. However, they saw only 27 camel herds, probably too small a sample for the use of such detailed statistics. At least the authors acknowledge that the results "should be viewed with caution." So far there is no wholly reliable information on camel numbers and population trends.

Based on estimates made during the 1990s in the three main camel areas of China—the Taklimakan, Gashun Gobi, and Arjin Mountains—there appear to be a total of roughly 400 to 500 camels. These camels now have legal protection in reserves. The Altun Mountain Nature Reserve, 5,790 square miles (15,000 km²) in size, was established in 1986. The Xinjiang Department of Environmental Protection set up the Lop Nur Wild Camel Nature Reserve, which incorporates the Altun Mountain Reserve, in 2000 (see John Hare, "Ghost of the Gobi" and *The Lost Camels of Tartary*). Its size is 30,031 square miles (77,800 km²). However, the total area under protection and management is 61,760 square miles (160,000 km²) because it includes the former nuclear testing zone near Lop Nur. This huge reserve was upgraded to a national reserve in 2003. There is in addition the 1,506-square-mile (3,900 km²) Annanba Reserve in Gansu Province, adjoining Xinjiang. To protect virtually the whole landscape for the wide-ranging camels is a superb initiative by China.

Once a part of the Lop Nur region was relatively lush, with a large lake and marshes. In the 1970s the lake dried up when the waters from the Tarim River, which flowed into it from the west, were dammed and diverted for agriculture. The environmentalist John Hare, after a visit in the mid-1990s, wrote: "Three water sources near the northern end of Lop Nur, which were known to be water pools for camels in the early 1980s, were dry."

An additional reserve needs to be established by China. Camels from Mongolia's Gobi A Park wander south into China's Gansu Province. There in the Dacaotan Springs area they encounter not only poachers but also many gold miners, who have polluted the ground with potassium cyanide. A few camels also drift from Gansu into neighboring Xinjiang and Inner Mongolia, mainly during winter. The Dacaotan Springs area should at a minimum be established as a strict reserve to provide trans-frontier protection for camels and Gobi bears.

It is known that the camels in Gobi A wander considerably within the park. In late autumn, following early snowfalls, they tend to move south to the Atas Bogd region, where they can obtain moisture by eating snow or drinking from seepages. In midwinter, during the rut, males and their harems tend to move toward the center of the park. However, no one imagined how widely camels might actually wander until Richard Reading and his colleagues attached a satellite radio to a female in 2002. She used a home range of 6,652 square miles (17,232 km²) in the ensuing months. Even this one figure gives an indication

Several wild Bactrian camels walk in single file across the Gobi desert.

of the amount of space camels need to survive in their severe habitat. They cannot thrive if they have to compete with livestock for sparse forage and water, as is the case in parts of the Gobi Park area. Furthermore, the growing season in the region is a mere 60 to 120 days a year. The rest of the time the vegetation is sparse, dry, coarse, and low in nutrients. Competition with livestock for this forage may well doom many camels. As I had noted, some camels we saw were lean, with bones showing beneath a slack hide.

Reading rightly noted in *Ecology and Conservation of Wild Bactrian Camels:* "Wild Bactrian camels are poorly understood. Knowledge of the species is limited, derived from only a few short studies, surveys, and anecdotal information. . . . These data suggest camel numbers are small and declining, and that camel recruitment is low." Matters have, to my knowledge, not improved much in recent years. So how many wild camels exist today? Given the estimates provided above for Mongolia and China, I would guess that the total number could be fewer than a thousand.

In a disturbing lack of awareness and cooperation between government departments, Mongolia suddenly opened in 1992 a border crossing to China for commercial trade through the "strictly protected" Gobi Park A, over the objection of the Ministry of Nature and Environment. Two new roads were built to the border inside the park close to the western and eastern edges. Truckers, however, took shortcuts through the center of the park and camped at the oases. These crossings were closed the following year after a public outcry. There are six military posts on the Mongolia-China border, each with about thirty people, and these all occupy oases and have access roads through prime bear and camel habitats. For several years the border guards received no salary and supported themselves by hunting wildlife. The seeming lack of active concern and cooperation on behalf of conservation by government departments is truly worrisome. Does the national park have a future? Some years ago, local communities could freely harvest reeds at oases for livestock feed and cut *Haloxylon* shrubs for fuel wood in what is now the park. What restrictions will now be equally casually discarded?

The park persists with the splendor of its wildlife intact, and it will certainly continue to do so as long as dedicated conservationists monitor problems and strive to find solutions that offer a secure future to all plant and animal species there. Any optimism of mine is naturally tempered by the impact of climate change, which continues to desiccate the landscape and dry up oases, and by the lack of good management that allows the incursion of miners and herders into even the core of protected areas.

2

Tracking the Golden Bear

Population size is believed to have remained relatively stable since the 1970s, but low reproductive rates, the potential effects of inbreeding, and extreme environmental conditions continue to constitute severe threats. As the population consists of fewer than 50 mature individuals, this taxon qualifies as Critically Endangered.

Emma L. Clark and Munkhbat Javzansuren, comps.,
Mongolian Red List of Mammals *(2006)*

Kay and I arrived back at Bayan Tooroi, the headquarters of the Great Gobi National Park, on May 12, 1990. We had flown to Altai with O. Byambaa, our new interpreter, and continued by jeep to the park to await our second jeep from UB with equipment and food. Park biologist Tulgat would help us capture and radio-collar Gobi bears in the month ahead. I'm happy to leave Ulaan Baatar, where the situation is said to be "unstable." The monolithic one-party state, established in the 1920s, has collapsed. There are now five parties vying for power, a recipe for political chaos.

I have had good meetings with Tserendeleg in UB. I donated various items of equipment, among them a video and still camera and a spotting scope, to his new organization, the Mongolian Union for the Conservation of Nature and Environment, of which he is vice president. He planned to head out with our jeep, our driver Tserendorj, and all our equipment to Gobi Park while we went by plane. Now we wait for the car at Bayan Tooroi. And wait. Byambaa finally gets a call through to UB. Byambaa is short, bespectacled, and reserved. He is forty-five years old and until recently was a lawyer for a labor union. He looks blank when I ask him about news from UB. Finally he notes that in the time of Genghis Khan the bearer of bad news was beheaded. I assure him that my response will be limited to frustration or perhaps a touch of anger. Tserendeleg is not coming after all, I'm told, and the car has not even left UB yet. Of course, I have no idea if this is even an approximation of the truth. The car may have gone on some private trading mission for food and other goods, as has happened before.

At least Kay and I are in the Gobi. A study of the Gobi bear is the kind of project I like. The animal is rare and beautiful, it inhabits a remote place, its desert environment presents intriguing ecological questions in need of answers, and it offers a conservation challenge. Other desert-dwelling brown bears live in Pakistan and Iran, but not in habitats that are as severe.

I wonder how the bears reached this corner of Mongolia. To the west of the park, visible as a faint, shimmering mirage on the horizon, is the eastern tip of the Tian Shan, the Heavenly Mountains, of China. Brown bears occur there, as I noted during a survey a few years ago. They are said to be of the Central Asian subspecies *Ursus arctos isabellinus*. Some of these bears may have wandered across to the Gobi in the past when the climate was benign with more rain and vegetation. At present the Gobi receives fewer than 5 inches (12.7 cm) of precipitation per year, and temperatures range from a blistering 115 degrees Fahrenheit (46° C) to a low of 40 (4.4° C).

The Gobi bears remained hidden in their desert domain until they were recorded by Russian and Mongolian biologists in 1900,

George Schaller scans the Gobi desert for wildlife.

though they were apparently not observed until 1943. Their range today encompasses only about 5,790 to 6,176 square miles (15,000 to 16,000 km²), mainly in the southern part of the park near the Chinese border. There a series of three desolate mountain ranges stretch from west to east, the Atas Ingen, Shar Khuls (or Shar Hulas), and Tsagaan Bogd. Each is a bear activity center with a number of oases. At least 30 miles (48 km) of desert separate the mountain massifs from one another. Even half a century ago the bears had a wider distribution. Their range extended to the Edrengiyn Nuru range along the northern park boundary and beyond, as well as about 30 miles east of the current park. In 1994, three bears showed up at the Dacaotan Springs south of the park in China. The various estimates of the total number of Gobi bears in existence today assume a population of around twenty-five to forty, making them critically endangered, even though they have been fully protected by law since 1953.

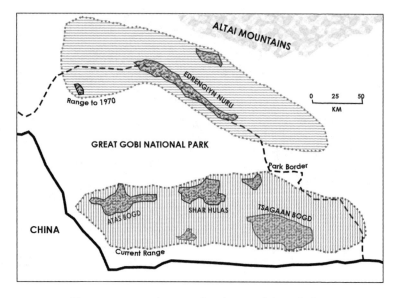

The recent past and current distribution of the Gobi bear.

Little detail is available about the lives of these bears, and I'm impatient to start work. Where is our car? Kay and I wander around. We watch the tamed wild camels, of which there are ten now. We observe which grasses and other plants the captive saiga antelope choose for forage. We note small flocks of migrating wheatear. We eat our usual meals of bread and thin mutton-noodle soup. Killing time. Tulgat informs us that a car has been sent to look for our car and its driver Tserendorj. He is coming alone from UB. Given today's unsettled conditions, it was a bad idea to send a lone driver in a car stuffed with valuable goods. Finally, after five days, Tserendorj is found. He is at a military base near the China border, claiming to have been lost. He will now go directly to the Shar Khuls oasis, where we camped last year, and meet us there. At least our telemetry and other equipment seem to be safe.

We leave in a jeep and a truck in the morning for the oasis, carrying gasoline and gear, and reach it at 5 p.m. The oasis lies along a dry streambed hemmed in by rock slopes. Tserendorj is not there: apparently he is still relaxing at the military base nearly 30 miles away. Angry, I send our driver Gantemur to fetch him. They return together at 11 p.m. Tserendorj is short, stocky, and bland, with white hair; he wears an ankle-length raincoat. Kay and I are up at dawn to organize our tent and all the research equipment. Three hours later, with the sun high, I go to check on the others. Tulgat gives me a grunt and sullen look as he turns over to sleep some more. At 9:45, Byambaa gets up and groans, "I'm very tired." After decades of being told by Russians what to do, they no doubt resent yet another foreigner urging them to work.

Later that morning, Tulgat demands a detailed explanation of the functions of all research equipment, especially the snares and items used to tranquilize and collar the bears. He is rightly concerned about the consequences if a bear is injured or dies. So am I. When collaring giant pandas and Asiatic black bears in China, I well remember the stress on us all until the animal had moved safely back into the forest. I show our team how the foot snares function. We then head out into the oasis and place a snare by a bear-feeding station. I scoop a depression and place the snare loop over it. Beneath is a trigger which when depressed by the bear's paw releases a spring that flips the snare up and tightens it around wrist or ankle. The snare cable is bolted to a log or other heavy object, which the bear can drag only with difficulty. A heavy-duty spring is attached to the snare's cable to soften the jerks of an agitated bear. Everything is then carefully hidden with leaves and grass. An innocuous few branches guide the bear over the snare as it tries to reach the bait.

The following day we drive east to the Hoshoot Bulak oasis and

Kay Schaller relaxes in the shade of a Gobi cliff during the midday heat.

Our camp in the vast grasslands of the eastern steppe.

set two snares and then two further snares at the Tsagaan Burgas Bulak oasis. As always I check the contents of the bear scats. I've tallied 179 scats in two days, of which 170 consist of pellets eaten at feeding stations. The remaining 9 are the ones of interest: two contain roots, one has green grass, two the remains of gerbils (a rodent), and two have tufts of hair and skin from ibex, probably scavenged. Scattered here and there are small pits made by bears in their effort to dig up the tap root of wild rhubarb (*Rheum nanum*), a favored food. I collect samples of this plant and several others for later analysis of nutrient content. After their brief hibernation from about November to February, followed by meager spring forage, the bears now need a good diet to regain their weight. Too bad they can find so little protein-rich meat.

I check the two traps in our oasis early every morning, content to amble alone. But to check the other snares requires a 62-mile (100 km) cross-country trip over rippled and rutted terrain. Tserendorj typically races the jeep along only to slam on the brakes at some obstruction, jolting and snapping our bodies until we ache. Wildlife seems to have abandoned our region. Once we observe two female argali each with a youngster, and once a khulan, all racing away from us. Hares here seem to rule the land. At least the weather has been pleasant, with a cool minimum 59 degrees Fahrenheit (15° C) at night and a modest 77 degrees (25° C) in the daytime.

On May 23 Kay joins our morning tour and brings us luck. We approach a snare site in the Hoshoot oasis, Tulgat in the lead. He stops abruptly and points. A brown bear lies quietly at the edge of the streambed, chin resting on a log. I retreat and prepare the syringe dart with the tranquilizing drug *Telazol,* the pistol that shoots the drug, and the radio-collar. The bear emits a plaintive moan, snorts, and chomps his teeth in annoyance when I approach slowly. When

*A Gobi bear peers from his rocky retreat, where
he has been resting during the heat of day.*

this does not deter me, it roars loudly twice and lunges, but the snare
cable jolts it to a halt. I shoot the syringe from 35 feet, but my aim is
low. The syringe glances off the log. A second syringe hits him in the
thigh. It is 11:13. Soon the bear's head sways from side to side, and
at 11:23 the animal lies down. After a few minutes, I prod the body
lightly with a stick. The bear is deeply asleep. It is a male, a golden
reddish-brown, honey-colored, and shaggy. Finally I have met the
golden bear.

Tserendorj removes the snare from the bear's forepaw. There is, to
my relief, no injury, not even a swelling. We weigh him on a spring
scale: 121 pounds (55 kg). He is small and probably not yet adult. We
then bolt the radio-collar around his neck. The radio is VHF (Very
High Frequency) and requires us to carry a receiver and antenna to
receive the line-of-sight signal. In open terrain the signal, a series of

beeps, carries directly to us over about 6 miles (10 km), but in this maze of canyons the signal will bounce from wall to wall, making it difficult to pinpoint the bear's precise location. We will have much daily hiking and climbing ahead of us to find Hoshoot, as we quickly named the bear (for the oasis at which he was caught). At 11:55, Hoshoot raises his head and rests, propped on his elbows. Kay, Tserendorj, and Byambaa retreat and quietly sit on the high embankment, and I stand screened by dense tamarisks. Tulgat, however, wanders near the bear as if testing his tolerance. Suddenly, with a harsh *woof,* the bear charges, but his legs are still wobbly and he stops abruptly. We all retreat to the car. Tulgat says that he has forgotten his camera at the trap site, and again approaches the bear. This time the bear charges, no longer wobbly, and bounds down the streambed toward the running Tulgat, but then veers up the hillside and disappears.

Kay and I are elated that the capture and collaring have gone well. Yet neither Tulgat nor, later, our Mongolian colleagues at camp show much emotion. This seeming cultural difference puzzles me, and I ask Byambaa about it. He replies succinctly: "Mongolian eat meat, don't talk much, seldom say 'good morning' or otherwise respond." But that evening at dinner we make vodka toasts to Gobi bears, and even Tulgat abandons his gloom and joins the communal gaiety. Later, from our tent, we look down the valley, where the setting sun sets the plains aglow and somewhere a golden bear wanders in the solitude.

Adult bears are a darker brown than Hoshoot, especially in the legs, and they may have a whitish crescent in front of the shoulder. Russian scientists have for years designated the Gobi bear with the same subspecies name, *pruinosus,* as the Tibetan brown bear. I have observed Tibetan brown bears, and there is little resemblance between them and Gobi bears. The legs and undersides of Tibetan bears are black or very dark brown, as are the ears and shoulder hump. Only

R. Tulgat (right) *and George Schaller fasten a radio-collar around the neck of a sedated Gobi bear.*

Annoyed at seeing our car after awakening from being sedated and collared, the Gobi bear bluff-charges.

the face is light brown. A broad white band extends around the neck and shoulders, and the saddle may also be silvery, especially in adult males.

We return to the Hoshoot oasis the next morning to reset the snare and bait it with a chunk of mutton. Two-thirds of the way there we climb a hill, the handheld antenna ready to search for Hoshoot. The signal is loud and clear, and we record the location. After resetting the snare, we return to Hoshoot, but he has moved away, the signal erratic among the granite hills. Tulgat and I then climb a high ridge so we can receive the signal well. The radio transmitter has a motion sensor which indicates whether the animal is active, walking or looking around, or at rest. Every fifteen minutes we turn on the receiver and record whether Hoshoot is active or inactive. We monitor him for four and a half hours, a fierce wind pounding us. Hoshoot is mostly active in one small area, possibly digging up wild rhubarb roots or cropping wild onion shoots. Back at camp, Kay has spent the afternoon leaning against the inside of the tent wall to keep it from blowing away. The guy ropes of the dome tent have snapped, and I attach stronger ones.

Tsand, a park guard who has just joined us, tells me that he has to take his motorcycle to Altai for repairs, and Gantemur claims the brakes in his jeep are failing and that he must leave too. No doubt they find life in town more fun than in our Spartan desert camp. I check the snares in our oasis, and after a lunch of tea, old bread, and jam head in the other jeep for Hoshoot's oasis. There is a fresh bear track, larger than the 7-inch (18 cm)-long rear foot of Hoshoot. There is no signal until I climb a high ridge and receive faint beeps far to the east. Hoshoot, it turns out, has traveled over 18.6 miles (30 km) in just two days.

The gale is so strong that pebbles on the plains rustle and at day's end my pockets are full of sand. We once again go in search of Ho-shoot, first to the place where we located him yesterday, but without luck. After much searching we receive a clear signal from a canyon near the Tsagaan Tohoin oasis. It was assumed that bears hang around oases most of the time and don't travel far from them. But Hoshoot certainly wanders widely, and I wonder if, as a young male, he is look-ing for a place to settle down. Tulgat and I monitor Hoshoot for eight hours while Tserendorj works on the jeep. Hoshoot was inactive for twenty-nine of the thirty-seven readings. A leisurely day for us all.

It is my birthday, and Kay gives me a chocolate bar as a present. Our search for Hoshoot is now part of the daily routine. He has trav-eled southwest across a broad valley and about 5.5 miles (8.8 km) up a winding canyon to an oasis with a few poplars and a great many tamarisks. There is a feeding station at which I find ten old scats and a fresh one with green grass in it. Hoshoot certainly knows his ter-rain, including the exact route to this isolated oasis. The signal shows that he is at rest up the valley, and we retreat without disturbing him.

The following week is frustrating; we cannot find Hoshoot no matter how far we drive or how many ridges we climb in search of the signal. Only once do we briefly hear a few beeps from an uncertain direction, signals bouncing around in the canyons. Our field notes are random: a fresh snow leopard scrape, a six-year-old argali ram killed by wolves, the tracks of a large and small bear together at an oasis.

But at least I find pleasure in ticks. I am used to ticks skulking in vegetation or clinging innocuously to a stalk of grass until they can attach themselves sneakily to me for a free blood meal. One Gobi tick species is different. Its body is large and burgundy colored with long yellow banded legs. It can run fast and jump, ideal for catching prey, including humans. It is disconcerting to be standing still and see these galloping Gobi ticks appear from some shadowed lair to pursue me.

When I stand still, a tick may run in a tight circle two or three times as if homing with its internal GPS and then continue its dash at me. I have sometimes retreated slowly backward. Some ticks would follow me for 40 to 50 feet before abruptly giving up and walking away.

A bear is in a snare again at the Hoshoot oasis on the morning of June 5. He is large and dark brown. The snare cable is bolted to a round iron car part, which the bear has dragged 70 feet (21.3 m) to the base of an embankment. There he has churned the sand and gravel with a paw in an effort to escape. Partly hidden by a rock outcrop, I inject him from a distance of 40 feet at 10:22. He growls when hit. Fourteen minutes later his head droops sleepily but he remains alert. I have underestimated his weight and given him too low a drug dose. A dose supplement sends him to sleep at 11:00. We try to weigh him, but my scale has a limit of 90 kg (198 lbs.), and this big male weighs probably at least 102 kg (225 lbs.). He raises his head at 11:25 but then naps off and on for nearly three hours. Suddenly he leaps up, sees the metal weight to which he had been tethered, and pounces on it with a growl. Tulgat is hiding by an outcrop only 40 feet from the bear. Perhaps the clicks of Tulgat's camera rile the bear, which suddenly charges. Tulgat runs away. The bear gains on him. But the bear veers aside when it sees our car, and Tulgat dives through the open door of the car, where we tensely await him.

We named this bear Genghis, for his strong personality. We did not then realize that he would display another Genghis-like trait—the urge to travel. We never located his signal again.

Hoshoot is now cooperative, enabling us to monitor him on several consecutive days. He stays in and around a canyon which in one spot has water in a rock cleft. Among boulders at another site are several shallow hollows in the sand where a bear has rested, ideal places in the shade with a breeze and a wide view of the valley. I pick up Hoshoot's signal, but he seems to be high up in a barren shale massif. I meander up and down ravines and over several ridges until suddenly the signal is close and insistent. I peer cautiously around a ledge. Hoshoot rests among rocks 100 feet away, only his golden head visible.

We now have some information about bear activity in the daytime, but what do bears do at night? Tulgat volunteers to spend a night with Hoshoot, and he records the signals until they stop at 3:30 a.m., after the bear probably entered a narrow canyon or cave. I decide to stay with Hoshoot the following night. I pack myself a pint of water, some bread, a flashlight, sweater, and air mattress, and, of course, the telemetry gear. I pick up Hoshoot's signal easily, but after a couple of hours it stops. After over an hour of searching, I literally stumble upon the bear. He lies on a ledge of a steep slope. Unseen I retreat and cower behind an outcrop to escape the violent wind. Hoshoot continues his rest, on and on. At 9 p.m. he becomes restless but settles down again at 10:30, at dusk. A full moon rises close to midnight. The sky is a river of stars, and the black mountain slopes glisten. The night is now so calm that I should be able to hear the soft tread of Hoshoot if he decides to come over and inspect me.

I revel at being here alone with the bear. A chilly east wind springs up, and I slip into my sweater. Finally, at 1:30 Hoshoot moves out, and his signal is very loud as he passes near me. He is heading south toward the feeding station. The signal vanishes. I cross the valley in the moonlight and climb a high ridge from which I hear Hoshoot still traveling until he vanishes at 3:00. I now emulate him, settling down to sleep. After three hours, I check the feeding station. Hoshoot had stopped for breakfast and moved on.

The car picks me up, and we drive to the Tsagaan Burgas Bulak oasis. I leave to check the snares. Loud growls and roars ahead. I see a large bear enveloped by dust as he yanks at the fallen dead tree to which the snare cable is attached and violently paws the sand.

The bear is molting, the long coat on his head and neck already shed except for the ear tufts. He has a lean, purposeful look as he glares toward me. I inject him with the tranquilizer at 10:25 a.m., and he is asleep within ten minutes. As I presumed, this is yet another male. He also is too large for my weighing scale. I note that one of his long claws on a forepaw is missing. By 11:15 he is alert but continues to rest until he unsteadily rises at 12:27 and walks up the valley. We never named him and simply identify him by his radio frequency, 950. Tulgat and I monitored male 950 for a whole day the following year, as we describe in our scientific paper "Observations on the Gobi Brown Bear in Mongolia."

On June 14, we waited near the feeding station at the Tsagaan Tohoin oasis. An adult male (frequency 950) was among distant granite hills from where we briefly picked up his signal at 2000 hours [8 p.m.]. At 0200 [2 a.m.] he arrived at the feeding station. At 0255 we heard a series of grunts and tracks later revealed that a subadult bear (not radio-collared) had also been at the site. The adult remained active around the feeding station most of the night. The first light of dawn was at 0515. At 0623 we observed him leave the feeding station, angle across a salt flat, stop to eat Ephedra for 2 minutes, and then climb up a steep ravine. He continued over a rounded ridge crest into a small boulder-strewn basin where at 0700 he began his daytime rest. He remained there, usually inactive, until 2100 when he began to travel away from the feeding station, and he was still moving away at 0115 when we lost his signal during a rain storm.

We've been in the field working hard for a month and are ready to return to UB. The temperature in our tent reaches 115 degrees Fahr-

A hedgehog in the Gobi desert.

enheit. We have closed all trap sites and gathered the equipment in camp. Byambaa complains that "rats" keep him awake at night. I think they could be *Meriones* gerbils, an attractive rodent with tan body and russet tail, which piles *Ephedra* twigs by its burrow for food. Actually I soon discover that the "rats" are three hedgehogs. I catch one for Kay to cuddle its prickly body in her cupped hands. It rolls itself into a ball, black eyes peering out, as it chuffs in annoyance. Put on the ground, it will explode by rigidly extending its legs and huff and puff, a startling intimidation display. Kay and I climb a ridge trying to locate at least one of the three collared bears, but all remain silent. In the lee of a cliff, out of the wind, we share a jar of cherries.

We return to Bayan Tooroi on June 3, a phase of the project finished. We have had a good team that worked a hard day and sometimes at night in difficult terrain to collect the first detailed information about the precarious existence of Gobi's golden bears. We learned that Hoshoot ranged over at least 108 square miles (280 km²). The big male, 950, roamed so widely that we seldom contacted him. His range was over 250 square miles (650 km²), his travels extending 30 miles (48 km) north to south. A male may walk considerable distances during his daily routine. Hoshoot, for example, was monitored twice for four consecutive days. His average daily straight-line distance was 5.3 miles (8.5 km), a figure which does not take into account winding routes along canyons and climbs across ridges. Why do these bears move around so much, seemingly more than would be necessary simply to forage? Is it to maintain their social network? Our activity monitoring shows that the bears are active on average 45 percent of the day. They may be active at any time, but are least so between 7 a.m. and 10 p.m., the warmest time of day, and they are most active during the hours of darkness.

The search for nutritious food is a basic bear quest. With their unspecialized digestive tract, similar to that in humans, bears depend on certain components of plants for nutrition. Bears cannot digest cellulose and lignin in a plant and can digest only part of the fibrous hemicelluloses. The soluble parts of the cell—the proteins, sugars, and fats—provide a bear's essential nutrients. The animal must be highly selective in what it consumes. I gave six wild-bear plants and a sample of commercial livestock food pellets to the Department of Animal Sciences at Cornell University for analysis, and the researchers generously provided the following information. Taking just the soluble parts and protein of each plant, the usable food parts that each contains amount to roughly the following percentages: wild rhubarb root, 35 percent; *Stipa* grass, 24 percent; reed rhizomes, 17 percent; tamarisk branch tips, 31 percent; green onion shoots, 69 percent; and green *Ephedra* stalks, 54 percent. Livestock pellets were 50 percent. Humans compete with the bears for the large tap root of wild rhubarb, which is edible, may weigh up to a pound when fresh, and can be ground into flour. Nutrient content varies, of course, with the seasons; green growing onions, for example, offer a better diet than dry grass. Wild rhubarb has moderate nutrients, but in exchange for about 0.7 to 2.1 ounces (20 to 60 grams) of root the bear must expend much energy in digging it up. The livestock pellets offer fairly high-quality nutrition that is easily available in season at certain sites, and it is no wonder that of the 365 bear droppings I examined some 91 percent consisted of these. However, the pellets are lower in minerals such as zinc, phosphorus, and other essential elements than the natural foods. *Nitraria* berries, which are much liked by bears, are only seasonally available. Because of lack of funds, the feeding stations were provided with pellets mainly in spring, when the bears emerged hungry from hibernation, and in autumn, to fatten them up a little for hibernation. Yet the bears are in desperate need of more of the nutrition that meat can best provide. Sometimes meat scraps from slaughtered animals are left by the containers, and on rare occasions commercial dogfood. But even these items could not be distributed throughout the bear's range because of a shortage of gasoline for vehicles.

Our research results have been of interest but fragmentary, and the golden bear remained in most respects a mystery when we left. Fortunately Gobi Park received much attention in the coming years. The United Nations Development Programme (UNDP) initiated a biodiversity project there in 1993, and a variety of research programs were conducted. But I was disconcerted to find out in 1994 that the Ministry of Nature and Environment had signed an agreement with a Japanese film company that allowed it to snare rare Gobi bears for no other purpose than to put in a movie. They did snare a bear, which already had a radio-collar, now nonfunctional, that we had attached in 1990. Wholly incompetent at tranquilizing and handling bears, the film team left the poor animal in the snare for two days before managing to release it. The Ministry of Nature and Environment finally designated the Gobi bear as a species of special concern in 1994.

I had been unable to find a reliable Mongolian biologist to stay in the field and monitor radio-collared bears and snow leopards before I left the country. John Man in his book *Gobi* (1997) advances one possible reason: "Mongolians are as responsible as anyone else when they manage their herds, but for fifty years Communism eroded the will to undertake wider responsibilities. Always, there was someone else, above, to take decisions. In the old days, pre-1990, you didn't need to look after a machine if it wasn't yours. So what if it broke? So what if you couldn't do your job? Someone would order a replacement, and you got paid anyway. Meanwhile, why take the initiative...?"

Thomas McCarthy, a wildlife biologist, fortunately contacted me about joining our research in Mongolia. As he wrote me in October 1990: "After several years in Alaska, six as a wildlife biologist with the state, I am now interested in pursuing a doctorate degree, preferably continuing to work with bears in a foreign setting." Unable to find a suitably trained Mongolian biologist with whom to collaborate, I invited Tom to join our project to study both Gobi bears and snow leopards. This he did in September 1992, as I'll relate in the next chapter. From 1994 to 1998 he remained for many months in the Gobi, sometimes accompanied by his wife and two young sons, as he conducted highly important research on these bears. Tom was particularly interested in finding out the size, sex ratio, and movement patterns of the bear population, as well as determining if it is inbred.

My approach to the bear study had been rather old-fashioned. Tom brought new techniques and sensibilities. Trapping these rare bears, he reasoned, is not desirable, for it causes them stress, potential injury, or worse. Information could be collected by noninvasive methods such as obtaining hair samples for DNA analyses. Mitochondrial and nuclear DNA analyses could identify different individuals, determine relationships of the bears within a population, note degrees of difference between populations, and find out the extent of their genetic diversity. To collect hair samples, Tom attached a strand of barbed wire about 12–20 inches (30–50 cm) above ground around feeding stations and bait sites. When ducking beneath the wire, a bear often left a tuft of hair behind on the barbs. Bears like to rub themselves against the bark of poplars and other trees, depositing their scent. A loop of barbed wire around the trunk at bear-rubbing posts also becomes a source of hairs for analysis.

Tom and his colleagues published some of their findings in a 2009 issue of the scientific bear journal *Ursus*. They identified "a minimum of 8 bears around the Shar Khuls and Baruun Tooroi oases, or about 50% of the animals thought to use those oases at the time of the study." The eight animals consisted of three females, four males, and one whose sex could not be determined. Genetic diversity was low—in fact, the lowest recorded in a bear population except for one in the Spanish Pyrenees—an indicator of much inbreeding. In a study published in 2007, also in the journal *Ursus,* G. Galbreath and co-authors determined that the Gobi bear belongs to the subspecies *isabellinus,* as I had surmised, and its closest relatives are in Central Asia, not in Tibet.

Concerned for the future of the Gobi bear, several Mongolian officials and biologists promoted the idea of captive breeding—a terrible suggestion for the bear's future! The small wild population cannot afford to have several males and females removed for a life behind bars. Captive management of bears is difficult, and there is no guarantee that they will breed well. Besides, what would then happen to any young raised in captivity? Young wild bears stay with their mothers at least two years, during which time they learn what foods to eat, where to find them, and how to navigate the intricate mountain systems to locate oases and water. I am also concerned because I had so far noted little interest and competence in the management of captive wildlife in the country. The bears are highly endangered, and any mistakes could be disastrous. The safest way to preserve these bears is to offer them a peaceful and protected life in the wild, helping them when necessary with nutritious supplementary food.

The situation for the Gobi bear has improved in recent years as serious attention is now being paid to it. The government, for example, designated 2013 as "The Year of Protecting the Gobi Bear." A company released a new vodka brand named after the bear *mazaalai*. Mongolians also seemed to have become more dedicated to fieldwork. As Douglas Chadwick wrote in *Tracking Gobi Grizzlies* (2017): "The Mongolians liked to work, always anticipated the next task, and labored hard to accomplish it. Everyone did his or her part. No one shirked, nobody grumbled." And a major long-term "Gobi Bear Conservation Project" was initiated in 2005 using the best and newest techniques. Principal investigators of that project include the former Alaskan bear biologist Harry Reynolds, the Canadian ecologist Michael Proctor, and the Gobi Park biologist Mijiddorj Batmunkh. Chadwick, a frequent participant in this work, well describes the project and some of its results, its team members, and the indomitable bears in his book. Many organizations, local and international, contribute funds to the project, including the Vital Ground Foundation of Montana, which is wholly devoted to bear conservation.

The project team caught a number of bears in baited box traps. The two heaviest bears, both males, weighed 268 and 304 pounds, and the heaviest female 207 pounds, all well beyond the capacity of my scale. The team attached a Geographical Positioning System satellite collar to each bear. Such GPS collars are ideal; the tracker can sit anywhere—in a ger in Mongolia or at home in the United States—and monitor the animal's movements. Of course trackers are deprived of the pleasure of scrambling across the stark Gobi terrain for hours in heat or cold each day and then not picking up the signal. The GPS collars are designed to fall off the bear after about a year. Even then things may not always go smoothly, as Chadwick noted. "Since May 2006, all scientists using GPS collars in central Asia have experienced problems receiving data from GPS-Argos satellites.... It has affected not only our work but all researchers using similar collars in their region." What country was jamming reception?

The GPS collars provided information that would have taken years to collect on foot. One female, for instance, had a home range of 198 square miles (513 km²) and one male, 959 square miles (2,485 km²). Females, as is typical for bears, seem to be more sedentary than males. Several males roamed between the Atas Ingen and Shar Khuls oasis complexes, traversing the expanse of desert between them. One male headed even farther east to the Tsagaan Bogd, a straight-line distance of about 124 miles (200 km). For comparison, on the Tibetan Plateau we fitted a Tibetan brown bear female which had two cubs with a satellite collar in June 2011 and she ranged over 945 square miles (2,448 km²). A collared male at the same time roamed over 1,975 square miles (5,117 km²) before hibernation four months later in October.

By collecting hair samples with strands of barbed wire and taking photographs with automatic cameras, the project team has obtained the most precise information on Gobi bear numbers to date. A total of twenty-two individual bears were identified, fourteen males and eight females; later the minimum estimate was raised to twenty-seven bears. Statistical calculations suggest that there are between thirty-six and forty bears. Yet after years of observations we still know little about various aspects of the bear's life, and research such as this must continue.

All projects for the past half century have confirmed that Mongolia's mazaalai is critically endangered and in high risk of extinction. Strictest protection is essential to ensure the continued existence of its habitat and water sources and of the animal itself. Yet in 2012 there was a bill before the government that included a proposal to open Gobi Park to mining. Starting in 2009, many bands of illegal gold miners invaded the park, and some were arrested. The bears are tenacious and resilient, yet they need further help. More effort must be made to involve the local people in the protection of the park, to develop their pride in having this natural treasure at their doorstep, and to help them financially by assigning a percentage of tourist profits to the communities. Some schools near the park already have Gobi Bear Children's Clubs, a wonderful initiative of the kind that will help the bears endure. The park guards must be provided with good equipment for their patrols, the bears need nutritious supplementary food during lean times, all wildlife must have peaceful oases without human and livestock intrusion, and the government must supply adequate funds to protect and manage the Great Gobi National Park. That's not too much for the endangered golden bear to request.

3

Spirit Cats

High above the lake, GS turns to wait; he points at something on the trail. Coming up, I stare at the dropping and mute prints for a long time. All around are rocky ledges, a thin cover of stunted juniper and rose. "It might be close by, watching us," murmurs GS, "and we'd never see it." He collects the leopard scat, and we go on. On the mountain corner, in hard gusts of wind, GS's altimeter reads 13,300 feet.

Peter Matthiessen, The Snow Leopard *(1978)*

One December day in 1970, I hiked up a gaunt valley within the snow-swept peaks of the Hindu Kush Mountains in northern Pakistan. There I spotted a female snow leopard at rest on a spur, her chin on a forepaw. She had a kill, a domestic goat, and in a nearby rock cleft was her cub, about four months old. I described this encounter in a 1972 article of the Wildlife Conservation Society's magazine:

I angled up the slope toward her, moving slowly and halting at intervals, seemingly oblivious to her presence. She flattened into the rocks and watched my approach. Once she sat up, her creamy white chest a bright spot among the somber cliffs, then snaked backward off her vantage point to become a fleeting shadow that molded itself to the contours of the boulders.… From another rock she peered at me, only the top of her head visible, but a few minutes later she stalked back to her original perch and casually reclined there. I was grateful to her for being bold and curious, because she was so adept at hiding that I would not have seen much of her without her consent. I halted 150 feet away and in the fading light unrolled my sleeping bag along a ledge in full view of her. Lying in the warmth of my bag, I could observe her feeding on the kill until darkness engulfed us. And then there was only the wind moaning among the boulders and the occasional grating of tooth on bone as the leopard continued her meal.

To have spent a night near the snow leopards filled me with enormous joy. After that I watched mother and cub off and on for a week, during which they offered me intimate and unique glimpses into their life. Here is an excerpt from my field notes: On December 15, "at 0700, the cub clambered about on the rocks 5 m from its mother. Suddenly it ran to her and touched its forehead against her cheek. It then fed on the goat for 40 minutes while its mother rested on a nearby boulder. Approaching her after its meal, the cub rubbed its cheek against hers, licked the top of her head and then vanished into its rocky retreat."

I sought to observe and relive such tender and delightful moments with snow leopards in the next few years but had no success. Some cats probably observed me with their pale yellow eyes as I roamed through their mountain realm, but they carefully hid themselves, knowing that the proximity of a human might mean death. I did obtain a fleeting view of one in the Himalayas of Nepal in 1973. During months of fieldwork on the Tibetan Plateau in China in the 1980s the snow leopards were only elusive mountain spirits. They tan-

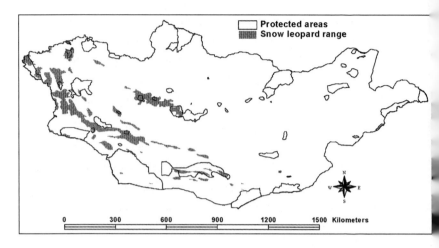

The distribution of snow leopards and principal protected areas in Mongolia.
(Map from T. M. McCarthy, "Ecology and Conservation of Snow Leopards,
Gobi Brown Bears, and Wild Bactrian Camels in Mongolia")

talized me by leaving reminders of their presence. A cat might stop at the base of a cliff to rake its hind paws on the ground and leave a conspicuous scrape. I noted an occasional pungent odor where a cat had deposited a squirt of mixed urine and fluid from the anal gland. Or it had deposited a tidy scat on a mountain pass seemingly awaiting my arrival to pick it apart to see what had been eaten. All these are visual and olfactory signs by which one snow leopard signals to another, "I've been here, join me or avoid me, whoever you are."

I recorded such signs avidly, happy to be in these remote and rugged mountains searching for these phantoms about which so little was still known. Snow leopards occur in twelve countries of Central Asia. Their range had been fairly well delineated by the 1980s. But only one intensive study had been done, research of nearly four years by Rodney Jackson and his colleagues conducted from 1982 to 1986 in Nepal. By radio-collaring five snow leopards, they provided

Snow leopard pelts decorate a government tourist lodge.

the first detailed information on the species. Considered endangered, and banned from international trade since 1976, the snow leopard is officially protected in all its range countries. But because it may prey on livestock, it is still trapped, poisoned, and shot in retaliation and to make a profit from the sale of its hide and bones. Mongolia has also been tempted to make money from trophy hunting, as I related in Chapter 1. Given the snow leopard's vast and often inaccessible mountain habitat, only rough estimates of its total numbers exist. Its potential habitat in the twelve countries is roughly 699,818 square miles (1,813,000 km²). The total estimate of snow leopard numbers is sometimes given as six thousand to eight thousand with 60 percent occurring in China. Mongolia's snow leopard habitat extends over about 38,600 square miles (100,000 km²). Tom McCarthy has calculated that Mongolia may have eight hundred to seventeen hundred snow leopards, the second-largest population after China. Yet the species is not secure. I remember visiting a government tourist camp near UB in 1998, and hanging from the ceiling of a large tent were seventy-nine snow leopard pelts.

The Survey, December 1989–January 1990

After completing our research on wild camels in the summer of 1989, we agreed to initiate a snow leopard project with a survey the following winter. On December 11, after a brief visit to Tibet, I flew from Beijing back to UB. Only three passengers are on the flight. Tserendeleg and the interpreter, Enkhbat, meet me. The city looks bleak, suffused with a brownish layer of pollution. Coal smoke is smothering UB, the toxic pall shrouding the city. Much of it originates from a power plant located on a spot where its deadly fumes will be spread over the city by the prevailing winds. The temperature is 0 degrees Fahrenheit (–18° C), and people are bundled in long, heavy coats, often with hats of fox fur. The Bayan Gol Hotel is warm, though its dinner of meat and French fries is cold.

Tserendeleg, Enkhbat, the snow leopard biologist Gol Amarsanaa from the Academy of Sciences, and I discuss a plan for the coming month. We decide to check on snow leopard distribution and abundance mainly along the Trans-Altai Gobi Range, which extends along the northern edge of the Gobi desert. If we find a suitable area for detailed study, then we could begin it in late 1990. Now to business. Two jeeps are essential in case one breaks down. Tserendeleg can provide one for this trip, but the project also needs its own vehicle for this and subsequent work. We hear that a secondhand Russian jeep might be available for five to seven thousand dollars. We also need to take into account costs for jeep repairs, fuel, food, and other items. It might not be easy to find a jeep on short notice, and drivers will be reluctant to travel in the Gobi during the winter. But within three days all has been arranged by Tserendeleg. The jeep has 42,000 kilometers (26,097 miles) on its odometer, and we can only hope that it survives the rough roads and drivers.

It takes us two and a half days to drive from UB south across the steppe and then desert to Dalanzadgad, the capital of Omnogovi Province. The problem is not that the distance is so great, but that the road, if that is an appropriate appellation, consists of a vague dirt track, or sometimes of ten parallel vehicle ruts churning cross-country. Visible to the west of town is a mountain range, the Gurvansaikhan National Conservation Park, a 4,908-square-mile (12,716 km²) area known to have snow leopards. A friend of Amarsanaa's invites us for a dinner of tea, bread, and a bowl of boiled mutton, into which we all dig with our pocketknives to cut chunks of meat from the bones. Three glasses of vodka each are obligatory by tradition at get-togethers such as this.

Heading west the next day, we cross a broad mountain saddle and descend into an outwash plain to the district town of Bayandalay. We inquire from the local leader about snow leopards, or *ir bes,* "snow cat," as they are called in Mongolia. He tells us emphatically that "the snow leopard is the most serious menace to livestock" and that "wildlife has declined because snow leopards kill so much of it." We ask how much livestock has been killed in the district during the past year. The answer is about sixty animals. How much livestock is there in the district, we query. About seventy-two thousand animals. I do a quiet calculation in my notebook, and note that livestock loss is less than 1 percent.

Tom McCarthy interviewed herder households, and his Ph.D. thesis offers more detail about snow leopard predation. Losses to snow leopards between 1995 and 1998 averaged 57 head of stock per year for the 105 herders he interviewed, or about 0.45 head per household per year. "Overall, 70% of snow leopard kills were large stock. Of the large stock taken, 53% were horses and 36% yaks. The reported loss to wolves was roughly three times the loss to snow leopards (168) during the same period. Wolves more frequently took small stock (56%), and the kill was composed of more sheep (63%) than goats (37%)."

Every household had until recent months been allowed to own only a few head of livestock. The remaining livestock was state owned, and each herder family was paid to care for a certain number. If a state-owned animal was killed by a predator, the family was fined up to three times its value. Private livestock deaths did not need to be reported. Now, at the end of 1989, a drastic change in policy has been implemented: all livestock is being privatized. This was to have a major long-term impact. From a total livestock population in Mongolia of about 26 million in 1992, the numbers had more than doubled within a quarter century, causing serious overgrazing of pastures, erosion of rangelands, and competition for forage with wildlife.

On our drive into the Zoolon Range, our local guide points to a narrow canyon in which he notes there is a water trickle at which wildlife drink. We walk into the canyon and almost immediately I find two snow leopard scrapes, three feet apart, with a scat between them. Farther on is a fresh snow leopard track, and I measure a forepaw at 3 inches (7.8 cm) wide and 3.7 inches (9.4 cm) long. There are more scrapes, single scrapes and up to four at one site, a total of twenty. I wonder if up among the boulders a snow leopard might be watching, puzzled by our curious behavior of measuring scrapes and tucking scats into bags. We find the skeleton of an ibex male, six and a half years old, his articulated bones and remnants of skin suggesting a snow leopard kill. But farther on we also discover two more ibex, a male and female, hacked apart and partially hidden beneath brush, the work of poachers.

All this information within less than half a mile (1 km) excites me. Amarsanaa, however, seems indifferent. He measures nothing, takes no notes, and ambles without stopping by a dead ibex. "I'm only interested in snow leopards," he says, when queried. I would like to know Amarsanaa's real interests, if any, and his perceptions about what we are doing and why we are doing it. I wish that he would show more initiative. Enkhbat, by contrast, is young, congenial, and a willing participant in our wildlife research. When not with us, he works for a Buddhist organization, which was recently established as part of the country's new "openness" policy. On the way back to town, we see several hundred Mongolian gazelles along the base of the mountains. I count 383, and there are more, obviously in rut, with males chasing females. No one other than me wants to tarry and observe them.

We had planned to check the wildlife in a large range to the north of us but do not have enough gasoline. The word *bakwa,* meaning "no" or "none available," is a frequent response to a request for anything now, when everything is scarce. We drive to a community named Hongopin, consisting of a few barracks and gers. We are told that no gasoline is available, and we should go to the county town of Sevrey. It's a three-hour drive over sand dunes on obscure, windblown tracks. On reaching Sevrey, it is again bakwa as far as fuel is concerned. But there is some available only 47 miles (75 km) farther on. Luckily we have enough gasoline in spare cans to get that far. The next morning our route traverses a bumpy gravel plain and meanders among hillocks. We then descend into a broad desert valley. Flocks of Pallas's sandgrouse in tight formation race past us. We find the gas station in the middle of nowhere, though not far from a salt mine. Gas is sold only for 10 liter (2.6 gal.) coupons. We have some, though they will expire on December 28, two days from now.

We continue southwest to the county town of Gurvantes. Towering behind the town is the rugged massif of Tost Uul. We move into the town's comfortable guest ger, grateful for its warmth in this sub-

*Biologist Tom McCarthy and local herder Amar examine a
snow leopard track in our Altai Mountain study area.*

zero weather. Mutton dumplings, tea, and camel milk are on the dinner menu. The television shows an Australian film of a boy hatching
an emu egg, and the news of a revolution in Romania.

At the west end of Tost Uul is a large valley, which we survey for
wildlife. There we spot almost immediately two small argali herds, one
with three rams, four ewes, and one young, and the other with one
ram, three ewes, and one young. I also tally seventy-two ibex, many
ranging low on the slopes, driven down by heavy snows. Most of the
ibex are in small herds with a male or two and several females and
young. Some large males are courting, following a female closely with
tail raised. And tracing the valley bottom we find the fresh tracks of
three snow leopards, probably those of a female with two large cubs.

In subsequent years, this region became the focus of two important snow leopard studies. Tom McCarthy, together with his wife
and two sons, captured four snow leopards between 1994 and 1997,

and he used the data for his Ph.D. thesis at the University of Massachusetts. They caught two males and two females, the heaviest a male weighing 90 pounds (41 kg). Tom placed a VHF radio-collar on each cat and found that their home ranges were small, varying from 5.4 to 54.7 square miles (14 to 142 km²). However, he experienced problems similar to mine: a cat would vanish for days in the rugged terrain because the VHF signal was not powerful enough to locate it. Later, from 2008 to 2014, the Swedish biologist Orjan Johansson studied snow leopards in the same general area, and he also radio-tracked two males and two females. He used the more accurate GPS satellite technology, and found that the snow leopards ranged over 126 to 237 square miles (327–615 km²), the males roaming twice as widely as the females, but all making excursions at times into seldom-used terrain. About three-quarters of their prey consisted of wild ungulates, principally ibex, and the rest of livestock. A cat killed on average once every eight days. At a conference in August 2019, Justine Alexander, working on behalf of the Snow Leopard Trust, reported that, when they left their mother at the age of around two years, female young tended to settle in or close to their mother's home range, whereas male young traveled widely before settling in new territory.

Now, however, we stop at a ger, where the herder tells us that he cares for about three hundred state-owned horses, of which snow leopards have killed two yearlings and nineteen foals this year and for which he has had to pay fines. Horses are often allowed to roam untended on high pastures for weeks. Hay is too difficult to obtain or too expensive to feed horses for the whole winter in corrals or sheds. This herder has a few foals in a low-walled corral about half a mile from the ger, an open invitation to a predator. Indeed, three foals in that corral have wounds from snow leopard attacks. Antibiotics are unavailable, and these foals may well die of infection. We stop at another ger. Our hostess takes care of 260 sheep and goats, and has suffered no losses to predators this year. She thinks we are hunters and is disappointed that we are not here to shoot snow leopards.

Gers are often scattered singly and in small clusters in remote valleys or are isolated on the steppe. Herder families treat all guests, anticipated or not, friends or strangers, with wonderful hospitality, even though most of them are poor. The average annual income of a herder family in the mid-1990s was the equivalent of only six hundred dollars, with which the family had to buy flour, rice, medicines, and other necessities. Nonetheless, whenever we come to the door, we are invited in without ceremony other than a *sainbaniu,* "How are you?" Milk tea is heated immediately on the central iron stove fueled with dung or wood. While waiting, we'll explain our reasons for being there and ask questions about the family's livestock, their livelihood, and the wildlife. It is also a good opportunity to exchange news. The ger is comfortably warm in bitter winters, the best and most innovative movable home ever invented. A cover of felt is tied over a round lattice of wood, and there often is a wooden floor. Cupboards, storage trunks, and beds line the wall, as do piles of neatly folded quilts. There is usually one or more thermoses, a radio and sometimes a television, a mirror, and several large cans to store water. Photos of family members riding a horse or camel, of children, and of festive occasions are posted on cupboards. Sometimes a newborn lamb rests in a corner. Dogs, however, are never allowed into the ger. We are expected to stay for a meal of perhaps noodle soup with bits of mutton and a cup of milk. If the hour is late, we are welcome to stay the night and sleep on the floor covered with a heavy quilt.

We spend a night in a ger belonging to Amarsanaa's relatives. The small ger is already occupied by two men, two women, and six children recently arrived home from school in town. Now the six of us crowd in to sleep with others in a row on the floor like the proverbial

A snow leopard peers at us from behind a boulder.

sardines in a can. The open skylight is covered at night to keep the ger warm, but even so the temperature inside is by morning often well below freezing. I lie in these gers sometimes at night, listening to all the breathing, and wonder what Kay and our boys are doing. To repay our hosts for such exceptional hospitality we leave some food or other items, and sincerely say *biala,* "thank you," and wave *biartai,* "good-bye," to the family. Being absorbed like this into a herder household is to me one of my most precious memories of Mongolia.

It is Christmas, and a snow leopard provides us with a special day. At the mouth of a valley we find a fresh track in the snow. It is –7 degrees Fahrenheit (–22° C). Amarsanaa and Enkhbat backtrack to see where the snow leopard has come from. I continue up-valley, feeling free to follow wherever the cat takes me. Judging by the track's size it is a male. He angles up a steep slope to a ridge, dips into a ravine, then climbs to a high ridge whose crest he follows a long way. I count scrapes and sniff his scent on a boulder. At a place where the view is wide over the plains, he sits down in the snow. After passing a rock face, he descends into a large valley and soon turns into a rock gulley, where I leave him. I have followed him for nearly 3.7 miles (6 km), counted fourteen old and fresh scrapes, and found one scat. He did not hunt and merely plodded along. Tost Uul obviously has a good potential as a study site. Now I sit down for a rest and to enjoy the solitude. In the eighteenth century the Tang dynasty poet Li Bai expressed my feelings well:

> The flocks of birds have flown high and away,
> A solitary cloud goes off calmly alone.
> We look at each other and never get bored —
> Just me and Ching-t'ing Mountain.

At dinner that evening in town, I explain to my colleagues that it is Christmas at home, and that it is customary to give presents to friends and family. I hand out a wristwatch, pocketknives, cigarette lighters, pens, and other items I brought. Amarsanaa borrows a guitar, and, displaying an unanticipated talent, strums it as Enkhbat sings Mongolian songs. We have canned fruit and pickles as a special treat with our dinner of sheep ribs and bread, and generous glasses of what they jokingly call *Ivan chai* (Russian tea), otherwise known as vodka.

We now drive northwest out of the Gobi desert toward the Burkhan Buuwdai Range, which I had passed through before on my way to Gobi Park. Along the road is the small town of Beger, and near it is the Uert Valley, which, according to Amarsanaa, whose family lives there, has many snow leopards. To reach that valley, we drive a few miles west of Beger and south up a gradual outwash plain to the base of the range. A track goes a short distance into the Uert Valley,

A herder woman cuddles a young saiga antelope, which she is raising.

Wild Bactrian camels and wild asses (khulan)
visit a water hole in the Gobi desert.

*Commercial government hunts once killed thousands
of Mongolian gazelles for export.*

A red deer stag bugles during the rut in the hills near Ulaan Baatar.

Several wild Bactrian camels walk in single file across the Gobi desert.

Our camp in the vast grasslands of the eastern steppe.

*Annoyed at seeing our car after awakening from being
sedated and collared, the Gobi bear bluff-charges.*

*Our research camp of three yurts or gers in the
Uert valley of the Altay Mountains where we studied
snow leopards. Our son Eric sits in front of the ger.*

Conservationist J. Tserendeleg examines a domestic yak that has been attacked and wounded by a snow leopard.

Herder Amar (left) and George Schaller hold a sedated snow leopard prior to radio-collaring it.

The herder Amar and his whole family wave good-bye (bayartai) *to us as we leave his home area in the Uert Valley after completing the snow leopard study.*

A large aggregation of Mongolian gazelles shimmers in evening light on the eastern steppe.

Several old monks have returned to the Gobi's Ulgyin monastery, which was destroyed in the 1930s.

Mongolian gazelles crowd around a seepage to drink during a period of drought.

Lhagva stalks a crouched gazelle young to capture it for weighing and tagging.

Kirk Olson (left) *and Daria Odonkhuu weigh a newborn gazelle young.*

and then we walk. Almost immediately we come across the tracks of two snow leopards descending a slope and continuing to a stand of cottonwood. On a leaning, massive tree the cats have clawed the bark to a height of 10 feet, the many scars showing that this is a much-used scent post. The pair continues up-valley and angles up a steep slope. From an elevation of 7,500 feet (2,300 m) in the valley, I follow the tracks to a pass at 11,800 feet (3,600 m). After a short distance on the ridge crest, the cats descend into another valley. There are more tracks there, but I don't know if they are from the same animals. By the time I return to the ger where we are staying, I have tallied over a dozen scrapes, found two scent posts on boulders, and collected four scats. I've also counted seventy-one ibex. Unlike the arid Gobi, these mountain pastures have marmots, an important prey item for snow leopards in season, but at present all are hibernating securely in their burrows.

We next survey the Bayan Sair Valley just to the east. Rugged near its mouth, the valley soon opens to high rounded ridges broken by rock outcrops. Snow leopards have been here too, and I counted about 240 ibex, including one herd of 80. A survey of a third valley reveals one fresh snow leopard track, a few ibex, and a number of gers. One ger has a fresh red fox hide and Pallas's cat (manul) hide hanging on the wall, and nearby is a large steel trap set for snow leopards.

We plan to survey several other ranges to the north and west for a few days, but I have already decided where to establish the project. The Uert and neighboring valleys have reasonably large snow leopard and prey populations, the area is conveniently reached from the Altai airport, and with Amarsanaa's extended family in the area we might receive cooperation.

We return to UB in mid-January, leaving the sparkling mountains for a city enveloped in noxious coal smog, our survey com-

*The Pallas's cat is widespread in Mongolia though seldom
seen, and it was once much trapped for its pelt.*

pleted. With Tserendeleg we discuss my schedule for 1990. Starting
in May, two months will be devoted to Gobi bears (as discussed in
Chapter 2), and from November on another two months to snow
leopards in the Uert Valley. There are lengthy discussions about equipment, payments, and preparations to be made locally for the work.
Survival Anglia, a British film company, would like to document the
snow leopard project, and we discuss this. Theodore Nist of the U.S.
embassy generously hosts a dinner for my Mongolian colleagues and
me. One of our outings is to the ger suburbs of UB, where I meet
a man with three live Pallas's cats destined for the Moscow zoo. He
presents me with a small bottle of traditional medicine to help my
general well-being. It contains the feces of a mouse, genus *Alticola*, in
alcohol. I did not test its efficacy.

The Study, 1990

I arrived back in Ulaan Bataar on October 29, 1990, ready to
begin an intensive snow leopard study in the Uert Valley. But first

there are the usual delays. Did Tulgat bring the telemetry equipment from the Gobi, where it's not needed while the bears are hibernating? Not yet. Amarsanaa is in UB and has agreed to participate in another project in December, just when he was expected to monitor any snow leopards we were able to radio-collar. Byambaa is again our interpreter, and we fly to Altai to meet Amarsanaa and driver Tserendorj with a jeep they have brought from UB. Late the following afternoon, November 7, we head out into an Arctic wasteland deep in snow. Tserendorj takes a wrong turn, something he tends to do, and we get stuck in a snowdrift. Lacking a shovel, we use an old car spring to dig ourselves out and return to Altai. The following day, we drive past the town of Beger and up the Uert Valley, past the few gers of the local herders, until we finally reach our proposed campsite, where we had been promised that three gers would be ready for our arrival. The site is empty. Soon a film team and my son Eric will arrive to work with us, and they will need a place to stay. We return to Beger to discuss the problem with Purendorj, an official who had agreed to help us. Two gers are delivered from Altai the following day, and the local herders generously help us erect them. On November 11, two weeks after my arrival in Mongolia, we now have a primitive base: two gers (one with a stove) and four mattresses, a pot to melt river ice, and a few other items. We borrow livestock droppings from the herders as fuel and a sheep leg as food.

The weather is fairly warm, around the freezing point, and this reduces my concern that a snow leopard might hurt its paw in the event that we catch one in a foot snare. Several goats should have been waiting for us, as requested, for use as bait to entice a snow leopard into camera range for the film team. None has been purchased yet. But a snow leopard solves that problem for us with timely cooperation.

November 12. Amarsanaa and I are in the lead, trailed by Tserendorj and herder Amar. Suddenly Tserendorj runs toward me waving an arm toward the slope and yells, "Ir bes!" About 200 feet away is a snow leopard lying motionless on a boulder. I had overlooked it. Disturbed by the shouting and pointing of my three companions, the snow leopard, a male, moves in a semi-crouch uphill, its gray-and-white coat making it almost invisible, a mere wisp of smoke. We examine the site where he had been and find a female ibex, her body still warm. She had been killed a short distance uphill and dragged here. Only a pound or so of meat has been eaten from around her groin. We have disturbed the cat at his breakfast.

We hurry back to camp to pick up a snare and other equipment. The ibex weighs 101 pounds (46 kg). She has no visible injuries, but dissection of the throat shows blood where the snow leopard had clamped its jaws to strangle her. Near the body are several stout willows, and we tie a leg of the ibex to one. Then we set the snare next to the ibex body and attach the snare cable to a chunk of old iron machinery to serve as a movable drag. We arrange some twigs to guide the snow leopard directly over the snare toward the ibex. I pick up my sleeping bag in camp to spend the night alone near the kill, as I had last done in 1970 during my studies in Pakistan. I have asked Amarsanaa to be back here tomorrow morning shortly after dawn, no later than 8 o'clock.

What happened the following morning is described in my book *Tibet Wild:*

> Cautiously I approached the snare at first light. The willow twigs had been scattered, but I saw nothing else until, up among the low branches, I discerned a dark mass — the snow leopard. After waiting nearly an hour for Amarsanaa, both the cat and I motionless, it was imperative that I release the

animal from the snare to prevent harm to its paw. I filled a syringe with the tranquilizing drug telazol and attached it to the end of a special six-foot aluminum pole. My approach was hesitant, worried that the animal might struggle and injure itself or react badly to the drug. The snow leopard remained in a crouch, growling, fiery eyes glaring, but made no move when I injected the drug with a quick jab into the thigh. Five minutes later he was asleep.

I lifted him gently from among the willow branches, holding his warm woolly body close, and placed him on the ground. Admiring the size of the paw, like that of a miniature snowshoe, I removed the snare and massaged it to get the blood circulating normally after being constricted by the snare. His fur felt sensuous as I moved one hand over his body and along the fluffy tail. He was about six feet long, nearly half of it tail. With a rope tied around his chest, I weighed him hanging from a spring scale. At 82.5 pounds, he was not particularly heavy, about the weight of an adult female, with males scaling up to 120 pounds, according to the literature. I fitted the radio collar around his neck. At 9:15 he awakened a little with a growl. After covering his eyes with a cloth to offer a peaceful recovery in darkness, I waited at a distance, binoculars trained on him to monitor his breathing. Amarsanaa finally showed up at 10:40. At 11:15 the snow leopard walked shakily uphill, stopping several times to eat snow.

Everything has gone smoothly, but somehow I am not elated. Are the data we will collect really worth so stressing the animal? He had struggled to free himself, biting at the willow branches and clawing the ground. Feeling guilty, I later climb the slope to make certain that he has fully recovered, and see him moving slowly along the crest of a ridge before vanishing after a glance back at me. For four days he does not return to his kill even though the radio signals reveal that he is still on the ridge.

When we get back to camp after releasing the leopard, Purendorj brings us a third ger, and the good news that conservationist Tseren-deleg, the film team, and my son Eric are due to arrive. And on the same day, I see vultures circling above our valley. Investigating, I note the tracks of two snow leopards which lead me to their ibex kill, a male four and a half years old. With the deep snow, many ibex have moved into the Uert Valley. I tallied 86 ibex in 9 herds during a casual walk, including 27 males, 35 females, and 20 young. The large males, ready for the rut, are impressively handsome with their long, sweeping horns, silver saddle contrasting with their dark pelage, and a black stripe to mark the edge of the white belly. At least 250 ibex may come to the valley off and on, ample prey for snow leopards.

The photographer Joel Bennett and his wife, Luisa, quickly settle into camp life, and they are keen to begin filming. Both are adaptable and steady, used to tough conditions after years of living in Alaska. They pin an Alaskan flag to the ger door. And I'm delighted to have Eric with me for a while. In his late twenties, he has just completed his Ph.D. in biochemistry and is taking a break. He also notifies us that he is getting married next summer. The radio-collared male had returned to his old ibex kill, and Joel has erected a tent in the valley nearby to film him. But he remains elusive, eating 46 pounds (21 kg) of meat and skin in four days without revealing much of himself.

We hear the radio signal up in a ravine. Eric and I climb closer. There is the snow leopard, resting casually in the sun on a slab of rock. At times he rears up and faces the sun, his eyes mere slits. Eric descends to alert Joel, who with a long lens obtains some footage.

*Our research camp of three yurts or gers in the
Uert Valley of the Altai Mountains, where we studied
snow leopards. Our son Eric sits in front of the ger.*

Remarkably tolerant, the snow leopard remains at the site for several days. Then we are distracted by a hurricane-like wind that whips through the valley and tears the felt covering off our gers, leaving them in tatters. Our herdsmen neighbors come to help with the repairs. Amarsanaa informs us that he has to return to UB. Since he has not helped with any aspect of the snow leopard work, and, in fact, has mostly gone off to visit relatives, his departure is no loss to the project.

Byambaa arrives in camp, and I'm delighted to have an interpreter around to relieve Tserendeleg and me of the labor of communicating in broken German. An important order of business is to plan for the future of the project. It is unethical for me to radio-collar snow leopards, Gobi bears, and others, I explain to Tserendeleg, if there is no Mongolian counterpart to track the animals and collect other data

Eric Schaller searches for snow leopards in the Altai Mountains.

when I am not here. I state bluntly that from my perspective Amarsanaa is unsuitable for the job. I will not try to collaborate with him anymore. Tserendeleg is tight-lipped: how to tell the Academy of Sciences that an American team member thinks that one of its staff members is not wholly invested in the project? However, judging by the attitude of some other biologists I have met, the academy may well be used to such a complaint. I now feel uneasy, not knowing if the project will continue.

Eric and I decide to monitor the signal of our collared male for three twenty-four-hour periods to obtain details of his daily activity. The sun reaches our narrow valley for only an hour now, and it seems sensible to lie in the warmth of our sleeping bags while we learn about the snow leopard's life. We check his activity, active or inactive, every fifteen minutes. The snow leopard has recently eaten, and on the first two days of our monitoring he sleeps much of the time, being active

*Conservationist J. Tserendeleg examines a domestic yak that
has been attacked and wounded by a snow leopard.*

on only 32 percent of the signals. On the third day, he becomes active
at 7 p.m. and remains so until midnight. He then rests until 5:00,
after which he travels steadily for three hours, and that day he is active
during 53 percent of the signals. It is so comforting and congenial to
be in a tent day and night with Eric, listening to the disembodied
beeps from a snow leopard, though by the third day I think mainly
of a good night's sleep. Day after day the snow leopard stays around
the Uert Valley, except for occasional excursions into the adjoining
Shar Hadny drainage. He remains within an area of only 4.6 square
miles (12 km²), partly, I suspect, because we provide him with an
occasional goat to eat.

One local woman persistently objects to our giving goats to the
snow leopard, saying we are training him to kill her livestock. At least
four other snow leopards inhabit our valley, and these, no doubt, all

prey on livestock. Free-roaming dogs also kill livestock, but such incidents are usually blamed on wolves and snow leopards. The five families living in the valley in 1990 reported to us that they have a total of 1,870 goats and sheep, 64 horses, 47 yaks, and 21 camels. Of these the snow leopards had during the year killed 11 sheep and goats (0.6 percent), 6 horses (9 percent), 5 yaks (11 percent), and no camels. All except the sheep and goats roam freely and unattended. Incidentally, Mongolians, unlike Tibetans, do not scavenge predator kills. For instance, one three-year-old yak had been attacked by a snow leopard and died days later in the valley of its infected wounds. A passing snow leopard ate a little from shoulder and neck, leaving a scrape behind as sign of its presence, but no other scavengers came.

I think the male snow leopard is beginning to accept us. For several days he sleeps in the same rock cleft formed by one boulder leaning into another. There he either rests in the sun or emerges in the afternoon, giving Joel a chance for a little filming. The ranges of snow leopards overlap considerably, and in our valley we know of a female with a large cub, another female with two large cubs, two males, and one adult of undetermined sex.

Eric reported a missing goat, and we investigate the site. Just as Joel sets up his camera, a snow leopard, a female, ambles across the sunlit slope just above us. She stops and casually evaluates us. Joel can't locate her in his viewfinder. Frantically he queries, "Where is it? I can't see it!" However, he later obtains some footage of her. "This is the hardest filming job I've ever done," he notes.

Slowly and with persistence we collect some useful information about these snow leopards. Our collared male consumed roughly 134 pounds (61 kg) of meat, viscera, and hide between November 12 and December 22, or an average of 3.75 pounds (1.7 kg) per day, about average for a cat of that size. During our forty-six days in the valley

A snow leopard lies draped on a rock surveying its domain.

Snow leopards blend well into their rocky realm.

we observed him on ten days for a total of twenty-two and a half hours, and recorded his radio signal on thirty-six days. What such data do not reveal is how much I savored my climbs through these mountains, with the sun glittering on the snow, and that I was able to observe a snow leopard at ease, his white chest gleaming among lichen-covered boulders.

As the country disintegrates with the withdrawal of the Soviet Union, so does our project. Gasoline can seldom be obtained without a bribe, and our vehicle is falling apart because of rough driving, lack of spare parts, and poor maintenance. Byambaa wants to return to UB, perhaps because he thinks that there is a devil in the Uert Valley, a large one wearing white clothes. In the 1970s, he tells us, there was a hunting camp in this valley, and when a horseman saw this devil he died soon afterward. A local official appears and falsely claims that we must pay him a fee to film and do research.

Our Christmas celebration is subdued, with roast mutton and potatoes for dinner. Amar and two of his children come by, adding a little cheer. I hand out small presents, such as a pair of socks to Byambaa, a scarf to Eric, and balloons to the children. Joel films a few more scenes—of Amar and me chatting, of me examining a snow leopard track. But we all know that Joel does not have enough good footage for a film, and he will have to return another winter to complete it— and that I have an obligation to help him. It seems unlikely that any Mongolian will want to monitor our male snow leopard, a thought that leaves me depressed at the lack of local dedication to the project. We are all happy to leave this cold, shadowed valley.

Back in UB, we endure meetings and more meetings about money actually owed (double-billing is endemic) and further equipment expected. Food shortages are extreme. Eric, to our delight, discovers several cans of peanuts in one shop. The hotel serves lukewarm rice and French fries limp as slugs. I do, however, meet Zamba Batjargal, the chairman of the State Committee for Preservation of Nature and Environment, who to my delight is an official who is actually familiar with conservation issues and genuinely concerned about them.

On January 7, 1991, Eric and I fly to Beijing, he to return to the United States and I to fly to Brussels, where I will meet Kay. Together we will revisit the mountain gorillas in Rwanda.

1992

Almost two years later, we met up with our team on September 29, 1992, in Beijing on our way to Mongolia to continue the snow leopard project. The team includes Joel Bennett and his colleague Hayden Kaden, there to complete the snow leopard film, biologist Tom McCarthy, who is keen to work on this project as well as do research on other species in Mongolia, and me; I am coming along on this trip mainly to help with the film. As we check in at the Beijing airport, Tom's belt pack is stolen from the cart. Fortunately he had already removed his passport. We did not know that the Mongolian airline counter (MIAT) expects unofficial "compensation" for handling baggage, with the result that ours was not on the flight when we landed in UB. Four days later a cargo plane brings tons of missing baggage. Instead of unloading it, the crew simply opens the cargo doors, and a mob rushes to the runway and clambers onto the plane. Baggage is tossed in all directions as each person digs around for something he or she recognizes. We finally retrieve ours.

Mongolia has a severe fuel shortage, and the government has canceled most internal flights. There once were daily flights from UB to Altai; now there is one a week. Tserendeleg informs us that Joel's pickup is badly dented, the result of an unexplained accident (actually, we suspect, the result of the driver's having been drunk while on a private mission to sell food supplies for profit). And my Russian jeep is somehow "kaput," he notes, using the German word. He has not found us a Mongolian counterpart, as officially required. We also meet Ravdangiin Tulgat, the Gobi Park biologist who had been very helpful earlier and who had agreed to monitor the radio-collared Gobi bears. He saunters into the room and is reluctant to provide information. It turns out that he has little, having spent only six weeks in the park during the past months. Partly this was no doubt due to difficulties of obtaining gasoline, but mostly, I suspect, it was due to inertia. We ask for the return of the telemetry equipment because we will need it, but most has been left in Gobi Park. All this is not an auspicious beginning, but it at least serves as an introduction for Tom to conducting a research project in Mongolia in these stressful times.

Our flight to Altai on October 5 leaves on schedule, so crowded that three people squeeze into two seats. The hotel is unheated, the weather freezing. There are still major food shortages, and we are lucky to receive mutton and potatoes for our meals. Food in state stores is rationed, with, for example, only 800 grams (28 oz.) of meat per person per month. On the "free" market the food is more expensive than in state stores. One kilogram (2.2 lbs.) of mutton may cost 60 tugrik; the average worker makes only 800 tugrik ($4) a month. Our well-paid driver receives the equivalent of two dollars a day.

About three years ago, a small monastery opened its doors at the edge of town. We stop there to receive blessings for our project. Ten monks are in residence, and they chant their mantras in a simple room with a small shrine, a religious scroll, and several burning butter lamps. As noted earlier, most monasteries in Mongolia and their contents were destroyed in the 1930s and the monks either murdered or dispersed. Only recently have small monasteries emerged again and elderly monks trickled out of retirement. The head monk here, named

Namsaraa, is seventy-four years old, a small man wearing glasses, a red robe, and a bemused expression. I give him a ceremonial scarf, or *khata,* deep blue in color, and 4,000 tugrik. He in turn touches my head with two sacred books and presents each of us with a handwritten prayer.

On October 8 we finally reach the Uert Valley. Amar has erected our gers, and each has a stove. Seven snares are soon set out, and we hope that it will snow, encouraging the ibex and snow leopards to descend into the valley. Currently the most conspicuous wildlife species is the gray-brown hamsters with furry tails that run in and out of the gers, plunder rice from our larder, and store it at times in my boots at night. Daily I wander up and down the valley alone or with colleagues to check the snares and bring water and hay to the three goats we have tied out to attract a snow leopard. Tserendeleg has taken a car to Gobi Park to pick up our telemetry gear, an arduous journey at this season, across snow-covered mountain passes.

It now snows and snows, and soon the snow is knee-deep as we trudge along to clear and reset the snares. The ibex have also moved off the high ridges. But where are the snow leopards? Did local people kill them to get us out of the way, as a Brazilian rancher once did to the jaguars to stop our project, which might have interfered with his illegal activities? One morning I see a bearded vulture and several crows up on the slope. A snow leopard has killed a yearling female ibex, eaten most of the meat, and vanished. Another morning I follow a snow leopard track, which passes a snare within 20 feet (6 m). We can do nothing but wait. A nearby herdsman's daughter is getting married, and in a neighborly gesture he has sent us flatbread and vodka (Magic Medicine brand) as a present. We have a short-wave radio and listen daily to the U.S. election news, rooting for Bill Clinton. So the waiting days pass.

October 27. The others are ahead of me when I see them wave. They are by a dead goat that has been almost wholly eaten. Tracks of three snow leopards, a female and two large cubs, are all around. And uphill is a snared snow leopard with the drag lodged against a rock. It's one of the large cubs, a female weighing perhaps 60 pounds (27 kg). Amar kneels with his face raised toward the snow leopard, folds his hands in prayer, and touches his forehead to the snow, paying tribute to the Spirit of the Mountains. I advance slowly to within ten feet of the cat, which snarls, ears laid back, large canines gleaming. Tom walks up behind her and jabs the syringe needle into her shoulder. Soon she licks her lips and within fifteen minutes is asleep. It is 10:55 in the morning. The slope is steep, and we worry that she might tumble downhill when recovering from the drug. I pick her up around the chest and Amar holds her hind legs. Together we stumble downhill to the valley bottom. There we massage her paw to improve circulation and fit her with the radio-collar while Joel films the whole event. At 11:45 the snow leopard raises her head and walks a few steps before lying down again. Finally, at 1:45, she heads steadily uphill and settles down under a rock overhang, only her long tail visible.

It's a tremendous relief that all has gone well, and Joel and Hayden have obtained their film footage. My job here is done. Tom will stay for three more weeks to monitor the snow leopard. The rest of us plan to drive east across the Gobi desert to check on several wildlife areas. Tserendeleg has taken the pickup truck, and we have to await his return. Tom climbs up toward a ridge on October 28 and meets our radio-collared female, and the following day she shows up with her sibling on a goat kill. The two have found each other! We collect all the snares, this part of the project concluded.

We are packed and ready to leave on November 1, when Amar invites us all to lunch at his ger. "You showed us how important the

Herder Amar (left) *and George Schaller hold a sedated snow leopard prior to radio-collaring it.*

snow leopard is," he toasts. "We'll do our best to keep it." The whole family crowds by the front of their ger, dressed in their finest deel (cloaks), sky blue, red, or black in color. They all wave, calling *bayartai, bayartai,* "good-bye." A wonderful memory.

We reach UB on November 18, relieved to be back. Our survey to the east had been hampered by constant vehicle problems. Tserendeleg has opened a small hotel, the Baigal, and I have my first bath

The herder Amar and his whole family wave good-bye (bayartai) *to us as we leave his home area in the Uert Valley after completing the snow leopard study.*

since October 4. I am booked to fly to Beijing on November 23. But Mongolia has reserved a surprise for us.

On the morning of November 21, the day Joel and Hayden are planning to fly to Beijing, they carry their many bags to the door of the hotel, where Hayden guards them, waiting for the tardy arrival of the car that is to take them to the airport. When the car finally arrives at 8:30, Joel and Hayden discover that two bags are missing—including the one with all 5,700 feet of movie film taken during our previous two months. After a frantic search, we spend much time trying to reconstruct the half-hour during which the film vanished. The police have been called to investigate, Joel does TV interviews, and radio broadcasts go out. A five hundred dollar reward for the return of the two bags is offered with the plea that the finder not open the packages of exposed film. I wander around near the hotel looking into garbage cans, hidden corners, and hallways and empty rooms in a housing project in case the bags have been dumped nearby, but find only a dead dog in one room. Tserendeleg consults a fortune teller who tells him, "Don't look. It will come to you."

This prediction comes true. The hotel manager comes the next day to inform us that someone has come to see us. It is a Mongolian man with gray hair, a fur hat, and a purple scarf. His name is Damdin. He carries a package wrapped in a coarse plastic bag and opens it. Inside is Joel's black film-changing bag filled with all his film and sound tapes; only his camera is missing. Damdin says, implausibly, that he found the package by the side of the road. No matter. Joel kneels and his eyes moisten as he examines the package. There is even Hayden's book *Rain of Gold,* an appropriate title for the situation. Joel gives Damdin his reward, worth 100,000 tugrik; Damdin's pension is 1,500 tugrik a month.

I have bought two bottles of red wine, the color Joel prefers, and in the evening we celebrate.

All of us fly to Beijing two days later. I'm content to leave but anticipate my return the following year to observe Mongolian gazelles on the vast eastern steppes.

4

Foreign Relations

Starting pretty well from scratch, the USSR had built a miniature of itself in Mongolia, not just industrial enterprises and livestock herding cooperatives, but urban developments like Ulaanbaatar city centre, Darkhan, and Erdenet, complete with schools and hospitals, shops and flats, buses, lorries and planes, cinemas, radio and TV—a complete socialist state, together with a Soviet-style party apparatus and parliament to run things.

Ole Bruun and Ole Odgaard, eds., Mongolia in Transition *(1996)*

When on December 25, 1991, Mikhail Gorbachev announced the "dissolution of the Union of Soviet Socialist Republics," Mongolia descended further into the turmoil that had begun two years earlier. Russia demanded a huge debt repayment, which Mongolia was unable to provide. Most Soviet advisers left the country in 1991, and all Soviet troops had done so by 1992. The Mongolian economy depended on membership in the Soviet-led Council of Mutual Economic Assistance, and the Soviets' withdrawal had a devastating effect on the country. The transition from a command to a market economy and from one-party control to a democratic system created administrative chaos, serious shortages in everything from food to fuel, high inflation and unemployment, and myriad other problems. Finding themselves suddenly dismissed and ignored, after being treated condescendingly as second-class citizens in the Soviet empire, the Mongolians rightly displayed a new nationalism and pride in their ancient history. Anything Russian tended to be spurned.

Yet with the departure of the Russians, new foreign invaders flooded into the country with such names as the World Bank, the United Nations Development Programme (UNDP), and German, Dutch, Danish, and other national assistance programs, as well as many nongovernmental organizations (NGOs) from Europe and North America. Each organization came equipped with a well-paid staff, most of whom were unable to speak Mongolian or Russian. Few personnel had much knowledge about the country and its immediate needs, an ignorance that made it difficult for them to spend their development funds effectively. Mongolia, in turn, became swamped with programs and money. The government became incapable of handling the dozens of nongovernmental organizations, much less supplying interpreters and trained personnel to act as local counterparts to the foreign advisers. (Aside from being required by law, such counterparts act as critical intermediaries between a foreign organization and the government.) Suddenly the country was yet again beholden to an alien value system.

I became part of this alien mob for two months in 1993 and again in 1994 when I was asked to assist a UNDP program, funded by the Global Environmental Facility (GEF) because of my previous wildlife experience in the country. This was my first such direct involvement with a large donor agency, and I found it illuminating. I had for decades scrambled for small grants to conduct fieldwork, but I had heard gossip about the effectiveness (or lack of it) of big programs while working in India and various African countries.

1993

The UNDP program's introductory meeting for participants opened on June 30, 1993, at the Ministry of Nature and Environment with a ten-minute speech of welcome from Minister Zamba Batjargal—although a number of invited participants had not yet arrived because the start date of the program had been abruptly shifted several times. Following Batjargal's speech the program manager, Walter Palmer, addresses us. He is a medium-sized individual of around forty, and he stands with legs spread, thumbs hooked into his trouser pockets as if ready to command an army platoon. The project has a budget of three million dollars, he tells us, and it will be divided into seven components dealing with biodiversity and human livelihood. Each of us will be assigned to one of these components. We have three days to submit a detailed plan of action for our component, including a budget. Three days? There is a puzzled silence. A thorough plan would take many days, if not weeks; we would have to visit and evaluate our designated sites and collect relevant information for a solid action and management proposal. Furthermore, UNDP has so far not coordinated the program with the various Mongolian government departments, and no interpreters and local counterparts to our personnel have as yet been designated. There are naturally many questions, but these are all brushed off in a defensive and irritable manner.

I am assigned to the component of reserve planning and endangered species conservation. Meetings on subsequent days help clarify how difficult it will be to make this program function effectively. Duplication of effort becomes an immediate concern. UNDP is establishing an ecotourism program, but so are several other organizations in Mongolia. Pieter Germeraad from the Netherlands is here to manage a reintroduction program for Przewalski's horses, a species of wild horse that was exterminated several decades ago but survived in captivity. Yet two other programs for their reintroduction are also being promoted. Then I discover that the UNDP will not pay our Mongolian colleagues any per diems, a daily allowance for their time in the field, if they work for the government. Since most are in some way employed by the government, they are in effect being asked to work for the UNDP without compensation. I am furious. Salaries for government employees are so low at present, often around two dollars a day, that some individuals have to become part-time traders, buying goods in China and selling them for a small profit in Mongolia or Russia, to support their families. The UNDP dictum naturally causes deep resentment, as well as reluctance to cooperate with us foreigners or to provide information about past research. Every Mongolian is well aware that the *daily* UNDP allowance for foreigners is two or more times higher than the *monthly* government salary. We object vigorously on behalf of our Mongolian co-workers, and several weeks later the UNDP does offer them a small allowance.

Several of us outsiders with similar interests draw together and plan how best to rescue something from this bureaucratic morass. Tom McCarthy, my colleague on the snow leopard research the previous year, is here. He has a research agreement with UNDP, but without explanation the length of his program is cut. The official explanation for this and other similar abrupt changes is an unhelpful "it's only an agreement." Two young and enthusiastic participants in the program, Jeff Griffin and Mark Johnstad, become our companions in town and field, as does Henry Mix, a German working with the World Wildlife Fund (WWF). Pareshav Suvd, who is fluent in English and German, gives us much valuable help and advice. I also meet S. Amgalanbaatar (Amga) of the Institute for Forestry and Wildlife, who has devoted himself to the study of the wild argali sheep. We soon share field trips. Badamjavin Lhagvasuren (Lhagva), the gazelle biologist for the Academy of Sciences, also becomes a valued colleague. He is tall and athletic, and his name card says "Around the World Trip on Bicycle." Slowly we're building a field team. But we also have to deal with Tsanjid, who is in charge of the country's reserves. Portly and red-faced, he usually dozes during our meetings. I mention to him that our team will visit the eastern steppe to locate potential new reserve areas. He looks at me bleary-eyed and says that he does not want me to go; he has enough reserves, and they will drill for oil and gas in all of them anyway. I stifle a response.

We need some basic items for our surveys such as maps. At the Land Policy Institute they hand draw maps with pencil on tissue paper. At the Geography Institute they sell us a slim but useful volume of Mongolian resource maps for thirty dollars, which I later find for sale in a bookstore for ten. All such expenses have to come out of our own pockets because UNDP claims that its budget is strained. Fortunately a team of Russian scientists has returned to UB. Among these is Anna Lushchekina (Anya), who has studied Mongolian gazelles since 1975. We quickly find out that the Russian team has various items of immediate use to our program, including excellent maps for all parts of Mongolia. They also provide a detailed management plan for Great Gobi National Park, relieving us of the need to produce a new one, instead of simply bringing theirs up to date.

We have no transport from the hotel to the meetings at the ministry and back. We can take a bus or wave down a private car, shouting *hoi-hoi,* "Stop-stop." Or we can walk. All methods are dangerous, especially alone and in the dark. Walking one night, Tom was surrounded by a pack of seven young toughs and politely relieved of his cash, sunglasses, and other items. Jachliin Tserendeleg of the Mongolian Society for Environment and Nature, a favorite co-worker of mine, is now most helpful in driving us to and from the meetings.

A number of my Mongolian colleagues show palpable annoyance and resentment toward the whole UNDP situation. Once again they are being placed in the position of supplicants, if not to a Stalinist political system, then to wealthy Westerners who hold the purse strings. The response of many individuals is corruption, a sacrifice of their moral resources and suspension of their integrity. Even some of my co-workers double-bill me, claim nonexistent expenses, skew the exchange rate in their favor, or other such indiscretions. I am saddened, my joy in being here diminished.

It is *naadam,* the annual summer festival. It has been seventy-two years since the country achieved independence, on June 11, 1921, from China, and Mongolians celebrate the anniversary for days. Our meetings have come to a halt, so I go to the stadium to witness the opening ceremonies. The stadium is half empty, even though Princess Anne of England, wearing a green suit and white hat, is present. The sun is hot. A band plays, and the sports contestants march in. Events include an archery contest, and fleshy wrestlers lurching around each other flapping their arms like the wings of lethargic birds. The crowd is subdued, lacking sparkle in these depressing times, and I leave early.

Finally, on July 14, after two weeks in UB, Jeff, Amga, the hydrologist, named Sumiya, and I fly to Choibalsan to visit the eastern steppe. The town depresses me with its blocks of gray apartment buildings, all now hollow shells, that were looted and burned as soon as the Russians left by Mongolians on a rampage of destruction based on revenge, nationalism, impulse, and greed. N. Ganbaatar of the local hunting association rents us one of his vehicles and the driver, Myagmar. We also obtain some coupons that enable us to buy gasoline. At a food store the only available items are rice, biscuits that look and taste like sawdust, and canned cucumbers imported from North Korea. Dispirited shop attendants guard almost empty shelves. However, at a nearby farmers' market we find some onions. After passing a demolished Russian army base at the edge of town, we are finally on the open steppe and my spirits soar.

The herder families are as hospitable as ever. We stop at a ger to ask for information and are invited in for a cup of tea and bits of dried cheese. I have noted that nearly all the diesel-powered water pumps scattered on the steppe have been destroyed, their machinery smashed or stolen. These wells are vital to herders for their families and their livestock, especially during the periodic droughts. I ask our host about this. His desolate reply: "The Russians built them. Now they don't belong to anyone." He is right. With the collapse of socialism, the privatization of communal property has proceeded chaotically. As Zamba Batjargal noted in his detailed and perceptive book *Fragile Environment, Vulnerable People and Sensitive Society* (2007), "Almost all dams and other construction for irrigation of pasture and cropland as well as thousands of wells and corrals and fences for animals were left without ownership and proper management." Given the lack of clear land titles, government control over livestock production and rules of rangeland use also ceased. Furthermore, the state-owned farms and cooperatives had provided important social services to herder families such as health care, education, and transportation. The government abrogated those responsibilities too. Without land tenure rules, "Every hayfield became a focus of local disputes between individuals and within herding groups," as one article in the excellent 2003 compendium edited by J. M. Suttie and S. G. Reynolds, *Transhumant Grazing Systems in Temperate Asia,* noted. And under so-called democracy all the people feel equal and can do as they please— even if what they do causes themselves harm, such as smashing water pumps. One Mongolian said to me about his countrymen: "They do exactly what they want to do, when they want to do it." Are these acts of moral conviction or justification for vandalism? I wonder how they rationalize such behavior, and I certainly do not understand it. But extremism reinforces itself; people react to one another's discontent. And most people have a tendency to adjust their moral values for their own convenience.

Mobility is the principal herding strategy that ensures sustainability for both livestock and rangelands. Herders on Mongolia's eastern steppe traditionally moved seven or eight times annually to provide the livestock with nutritious forage and ensure that the animals stored ample fat deposits to survive the long and lean winter and spring months. The collapse of institutional regulations led many herders to abandon their traditional ways as well, resulting in overstocking of rangelands and desertification, especially near towns, where the herders tend to gather these days. Many herders who had moved to towns to escape the regulations of the old negdels now returned to the land, often to raise goats because the wool brought premium prices on the international markets. Without controls, livestock numbers boomed. There were an estimated 14 million head of livestock at independence in 1924, and about 26 million when the Russians left in 1992. By 2017, "The number of livestock exceeded 70 million," as reported in the superb study edited by Undarmaa Jamsran, Kenji Tamura, Natsagdorj Luvsan, and Norikazu Yamanaka, *Rangeland Ecosystems of Mongolia.* These ever-increasing livestock numbers carry with their success also their ultimate destruction.

Rangeland degradation is a critical issue in Mongolia, and Mongolians need to reestablish a balance between grazing lands and livestock. When, as now in 1993, livestock ownership is private and pastures are public, herders have no incentive to manage and improve rangelands or to use them sustainably. Land tenure reform is an imperative.

We reach the county town of Matad. Its 240 families lack electricity. The local wildlife warden is unable to meet us because he is drunk. An official stops by our small hotel and warns us to be careful. The sole policeman in town was recently beaten up by a local gang. We eat our dinner of noodles and mutton by candlelight. Our driver, Myagmar, has already removed the door handles from the car to make it more difficult to steal, and now he will drive it far into the steppe and sleep in it to prevent it from being vandalized in town.

Over the next few days we drive on across the great steppe. Many Mongolian gazelle flee from us, some in herds of five hundred or more. I note that now, just after the birth season, about two-thirds of the females have young at heel, a successful year. The steppe once again takes possession of me, and I want to stride across its spacious beauty beneath the crystal clear sky toward the horizon. But we continue on, taking note of four wolf pups at a den, several great bustards, elegant white-naped cranes in a marshy spot, and other fleeting visions. We make a large loop and head back toward Choibalsan. At a county town we try to buy gasoline. *Bakwa,* none. Now we must return, and on July 24 we are back in town ready to continue on to UB.

The Russian team had asked me to join them on a survey across the Gobi, and I had accepted with pleasure. The team had stored two massive GAZ-66 trucks (Gorkiy Auto Works) in UB awaiting its return. Spare wheels and tires have in the meantime been stolen. We set off in two trucks and a jeep, fifteen of us including three Russian drivers. The gazelle expert Anya is the designated leader, although Peter Gunin of the Russian Academy of Sciences is actually in charge. Also from the academy are the geomorphologist Anatoly Preschepa, who studies landscapes and terrain, and the botanist Nikolai Sleminev. Gray-haired Mikhail Samsonov, with his excellent English, is interpreter for those who speak little or no Russian or English. Jeff

The empty shells of Russian apartment buildings and a damaged statue of Lenin in the town of Saynshand.

Griffin and I are the Americans, later joined briefly by Steve Kohl of the U.S. Fish and Wildlife Service. John Hare is tall, lean, and British, and he works with the U.N. Environment Programme. A wild camel enthusiast, he will later survey these animals in the deserts of China. Amga is one of several Mongolians on our team, as are Sarantuya and Dashzeveg, both graduate students at the Academy. It is a large, interesting, and diverse group.

We leave UB and drive toward Bayan Tooroi, the Gobi Park headquarters. In the evening we pull off the road to set up camp on a meadow. The Russian team has organized everything with marvelous efficiency. Tarps are spread on the ground, and sleeping gear is placed on one, personal packs on a second, and food boxes on a third, all within easy reach from the back of one truck. Our first duty is to erect a large kitchen tent with table and chairs. Two team members have already been designated as cooks, and we are served potato soup and bread. Sitting around the table, the Russians sing, with Mikhail contributing his deep baritone. They look dreamy, and the songs are full of nostalgia about "my beloved Moscow" and "my beloved country." Anya orders us to bed at eleven. We have already erected our personal tents. In the morning, she notes, we will clean the campsite. "There must be nothing left, not even a cigarette butt." I appreciate such care.

Late the following afternoon we reach the Tuuya River, which flows into the shallow lake Orog Nuur. Usually the river is dry or is just a trickle. Today we face a milky-brown flood rushing along several channels. Heavy rains fell on the Gobi last year, but rains this year are the heaviest on record since 1938. Two trucks are submerged in the river up to their hoods, trying to reach the town visible on the other shore. I know one of the drivers. He tells me that they've been here three days, for the townspeople refused to pull them out with their tractor citing lack of diesel. I surmise that the town has ample diesel—for a price. I give the driver seven dollars, and the tractor is suddenly available for the following day.

In the morning our team lines up on the riverbank and tosses pebbles into the water to gauge its depth. Impatiently I wade in to find a suitable fording place and John Hare joins me. There is no problem except for one deep channel. We locate a good route with water only up to our waists and the river bottom quite solid. We wave the first truck on, pointing out the precise route. Whatever is in the driver's mind, he veers sharply off course and plows into a deep hole. The water is to the top of the hood and inside the cabin. Peter, Anya, Dashzeveg, and the driver clamber onto the roof of the truck. Fortunately our other truck manages to pull the submerged one out. Several food boxes are soaked, turning the sugar, noodles, biscuits, and cereal into a soggy mess.

The road descends into the Gobi desert. The rains have transformed it from drab gray and brown into a sparkling green expanse. Nikolai the botanist is ecstatic. He points to a seedling of the shrub *Reaumuria* and notes that he last saw one in 1978. The saltwood shrub *Haloxylon* also has seedlings. Seeds may lie dormant for many years awaiting rain. Nikolai shows us the succulent leaves of *Zygophyllum* and notes that they are used to cure liver problems; pointing to the green twigs of *Ephedra*, he says they can terminate pregnancy. There are expanses of wild onion, and we gather some to flavor our meals.

We finally arrive in Bayan Tooroi. The name means "rich in poplars," and the rain-soaked trees are a richer dark green than I've ever seen. We are greeted by the new park director, Ayurzanya Avirmed, who is, we have been told, volatile and erratic. He is actively cool toward our Russian team members and rudely refuses to speak Russian even though he is perfectly familiar with the language. Mongolians told me that at another meeting he announced, "English is the language now." His attitude places a burden on the translators, creates tension, and reduces cordiality.

I had planned to check on the tame wild camels to make certain that, as we had recommended, they have been completely separated from the domestic camels to prevent further hybridization. Avirmed is evasive in his answers to my questions. Suspicious, I wander quietly around the area. There are six wolves housed in a small, filthy enclosure. I find out that they will be killed to study the use of wolf tongues as a cure for stomach cancer. I also note that the camels are not separated; they are being managed as carelessly as before.

We head into the park, driving steadily, the landscape merely passing by. The Shar Khuls oasis is our goal for the night, and we camp on the same site where my tent stood previously. The wildlife guard Choijun is with us. He and I worked together before on the

Gobi bear project. Now we amble around the oasis to look for bear scats. Because of all the green vegetation, the park personnel are not feeding livestock pellets to the bears this year. We find several scats containing purple *Nitraria* berries and green grass. By eating berries such as these, the bears no doubt help distribute the seeds via their feces to new oases. As we continue our trip our route takes us south to the China border. Where are the wild camels? We find the tracks of only one small herd. The camels must have gathered in the western part of the park. But we are heading northeast to the small community of Ekhin Gol. It consists of about twenty gers, several barracks, and a small hotel. To my surprise we meet up with an expedition that includes an elderly Russian botanist, Tamara Kazantseva from Saint Petersburg. The reunion is exuberant. A goat is slaughtered and boiled, and toasts and sentimental songs go on far into the night. After that, we have a day of rest.

Sarantuya and I have kitchen duty. Lunch consists of leftover goat and a potato-and-carrot soup. A local wildlife guard, Zekhuu, joins us. He has lived here for the entire sixty-eight years of his life, and I query him about wildlife. Gobi bears were abundant in this region in the 1940s, he relates, but only one has been seen since 1989. Wildlife has decreased greatly since serious droughts began in 1980. Various springs in the Ekhin Gol area and elsewhere have dried up. We both hope that all the oases will revive with the current heavy rains.

I now anticipate a leisurely trip east across the Gobi, checking wildlife in valleys and hill ranges and evaluating sites for possible reserves. But we roar on for mile after mile with only occasional halts. Adjoining Gobi Park to the east is the Tost Uul Nature Reserve, consisting of a series of rocky ranges and wide valleys. As we drive up one of these valleys, I look around again with interest. In 1989, I had found snow leopard spoor here. But we continue steadily on. Anya and I complain to Peter Gunin that we are not even stopping to count the occasional gazelle herd. Our main designated survey area is east of the town of Dalanzadgad, and we bypass it completely, reaching UB on August 22. Disgruntled about the poorly managed UNDP program, I am now further frustrated by this hurried Russian tour. After reporting to the ministry and writing a brief summary of our trips, I head back to the United States.

I muse about the behavior of Mongolians as I sit during the long hours on the flight home. I wonder how their past and recent history of upheavals have shaped their attitudes, a past of Mongols invading other countries and being invaded, of a people wantonly destroying its own legacy, such as the monasteries, demolished in the 1930s, and more recently the many buildings used by Russians, now reduced to rubble. Mongolia seems to have abrogated its collective social responsibility when it regained its freedom after the departure of the Russians. I realize that most countries, past and present, have descended into moral darkness, giving in to political and religious fanaticism, at some time in their history, that the world is an archive of atrocities. What precipitates this in human nature, what divisive social stresses? Is it that a feeling for the humanity of others ceases outside of one's own group or tribe, or even within a group, because of economic disparity, contempt for social differences, a race-baiting leader, or some other reason that provides a moral "excuse" for indiscriminate violence and various forms of savage depravity? I have no answer. But history overflows with examples of similar brutality.

Tribes of indigenous Americans were decimated by the military and evicted from their homelands in North America by settlers from the seventeenth century on. At that time too and continuing into this century, the indigenous tribes in Brazil and other Latin American countries were hunted down, massacred, and taken into slavery by rubber tappers, gold seekers, settlers, loggers, drug traffickers, and others who wanted their land or other resources, all with impunity, regardless of laws. In recent decades murderous majorities have initiated pogroms against minorities in various parts of the world for religious, tribal, political, nationalistic, and ethnic reasons. The rumors and lies and hate speech of bigoted demagogues, their deceits, propaganda, and hidden agendas often are at the root of rebellions. These have stimulated rage, mob violence, and ferocious persecution toward minorities and precipitated unpredictable tribal rivalries and feuds, especially during times of instability, apprehension over economic and other threats to traditional ways of life, corruption, and revulsion against foreign influences. The mass murders of minorities in Germany and the Soviet Union during the past century come to mind, as do the atrocities of colonial powers toward their subjects, as, for example, the Belgians in the Congo and the Germans in Namibia. In 1932–1933, a famine instigated by Stalin killed about 4 million Ukrainians, and in 1941 the German and Ukrainian military executed over 33,000 Jews near Kiev. Horrendous tribal wars have raged and continue to rage, in part as an aftermath of colonialism, within countries and territories whose maimed societies feel deprived of a clear identity, in Angola, Uganda, Rwanda, Sudan, Algeria, Liberia, Lebanon, and elsewhere. Religious minorities, whether Muslim, Buddhist, Hindu, or Sikh, have been or are being persecuted in southern Asia, in Pakistan, India, Myanmar, and Sri Lanka, as well as in several countries of the Middle East. Be kind only to those who believe as we do is all too often the arrogant and cruel principle of a religion. Foreign interventions in other nations have accentuated political and social instability, recent examples being the monstrous slaughter of the Vietnamese by the United States, decade-long wars of terror and destruction in Afghanistan, Syria, and Iraq, and the persistent civil warfare in Yemen for which the United States, France, Iran, and Saudi Arabia are providing weapons directly or indirectly to the combatants. Strife seems to be an origin of all major change.

It would seem that in Mongolia both political and economic stresses, as well as erosion of self-esteem after years of subordination to Russia, have dislocated the country's moral norms. Suddenly released to make their own decisions, many individuals decided on destruction. Social stresses may also have been involved. Most city dwellers were until recently used to the freedom and close relationships within their nomad society, but now, in 1993, they are crowded together without a sense of place, away from Great Father Sky and Mother Earth, and they have rebelled. Further exacerbating the situation is a severe lack of jobs, endemic bribery and corruption, and a devotion to vodka. Yet the people have a great capacity for basic goodness, as I was so often shown. Whatever the complex reasons, such reflections turned my mind almost automatically to Genghis Khan, the famed (or infamous) twelfth-century conqueror and destroyer. During his lifetime (ca. 1162–1227) he founded what became the largest contiguous land empire in history. In the recent Soviet times his image was banished in Mongolia, but now he has been resurrected and is revered as the "father of the country" and its culture.

Genghis (né Temujin) was born in northeast Mongolia. Even in his youth there was "fire in his eyes and light in his face," according to a fifteenth-century compilation, "The Secret History of the Mongols." Temujin's father was murdered, and the family was torn apart by sibling rivalry between Temujin and his half-brother Begter, whom Temujin murdered. When Temujin grew up he took over the leadership of his small tribe, then united all the neighboring tribes, more than twenty-five "hordes," under his command. At a great assembly of tribal chiefs in 1206 he was appointed khan ("strong man"), and added to this was the Chinese word *ching*, "chief," and thus he became Chinggis, or Genghis, Khan. Unity was essential in dealing with internal social and economic stresses at that time. These included a long period of drought in the twelfth century that created intense struggles for pastureland. With dreams of an empire, he built alliances and created a cavalry of mounted warriors. He led this army westward, each warrior armed with a lance, sword, and powerful bow and arrow, rampaging across what is now Iraq, Iran, Afghanistan, Ukraine, and western Russia in an unrestrained exertion of power. He died on the way back to Mongolia in the Gansu Province of China. His remains were carried back to Mongolia, though his burial site is unknown. He left a legacy of massacres for any city that opposed him, such as Herat in Afghanistan in 1221, or that did not offer total loyalty. "No eye remained open to cry for the dead," it was said in Herat. In Bukhara, now located in Uzbekistan, an eyewitness reported, "They came, they uprooted, they burned, they slew, they despoiled, they departed."

Yet Genghis Khan also had some enlightened ideas: he banned torture and granted religious freedom. In Mongolia he decreed the Ikh Zasag Khuul (Law of Great Assembly) in 1206, a hunting law which, for example, forbade the killing of wildlife from March to October during the breeding season of many species, and he prohibited the pollution of water and destruction of soil because these were essential to the lives of nomadic herders. Such ideas should be heeded by today's Mongolians.

Genghis had appointed his son Ogodai (1186–1241) to succeed him. Although Ogodai continued the conquests, his abiding interest appeared to be alcohol, such as vodka and *koumiss,* made of fermented mare's milk. He built a new capital in Mongolia and named it Karakoram, but it was destroyed by Chinese invaders in 1388. The Flemish Franciscan monk William of Rubruck visited Karakoram in 1254 and had an interview with the Great Khan Mongka, or Mangu, who ruled from 1251 to 1259. Rubruck in his journal noted that "Mangu himself appeared to me tipsy." The tradition of Ogodai has apparently continued.

Kublai Khan (1215–1294), the grandson of Genghis, extended Mongolia's control over much of China and established there the Yuan Dynasty, which lasted from 1271 to 1368. The first ruler of the Ming Dynasty (1368–1644) drove the Mongols back to Mongolia. Then, for half a century, China and Mongolia fought each other, while Mongolia also split into endless factions resulting in years of internal rebellions and civil wars. Wherever they went, Mongolians proved to be good at conquering but not at providing a steady rule. Taking advantage of Mongolia's civil war, Emperor Yong Le invaded the country in 1410, and Mongolia became a vassal state of China, paying annual tribute. In 1449, Mongolia invaded China again, but, as so often, the attackers were disunited and fought one another. However, the close contact between the two peoples stimulated cultural exchanges and alliances. Finally, by the mid-1900s, some years after the end of China's last dynasty, the Qing, in 1911, China and its Russian-dominated neighbor were at peace.

The conflict between the agricultural Chinese and the pastoral and nomadic Mongols was also based on a more subtle relationship. Each considered the other's livelihood inferior, yet the two opposing cultures needed each other. The Mongolians required metals and grain, and the Chinese needed livestock, hides, and wool. In addition to the aggressive and defensive frontier policies, they developed trading rights, negotiated peace deals after raids, and engaged in diplomacy, bribery, subsidies, alliances, and other nonviolent exchanges.

As I thought about my Mongolian colleagues, it seemed to me that the women tended to be more cheerful, to work harder, and to show more social responsibility than the men. In this, too, it appears that not much has changed. When the pope's envoy from Rome visited the Mongols in the thirteenth century, he found, as quoted in Thomas Barfield's *The Perilous Frontier,* that "the men do nothing but occupy themselves with their arrows and to a small extent look after their herds.... All the work rests on the shoulders of the women; they make the fur coats, clothes, bootlegs, and everything else made from leather. They also drive the carts and mend them, load the camels, and are very quick and efficient in their work."

Such similarities notwithstanding, there have been monumental changes since the 1950s. The forceful raiding across frontiers has disappeared (but not the economic raiding) and with it the ideology of conquest. Mongolia's traditional pastoral culture can persist if the country retains a balance between its environment and development to ensure a healthy future for everyone. In the words of the fourteenth Dalai Lama: "I believe that at the most fundamental level our nature is compassionate, and that cooperation, not conflict, lies at the heart of the basic principles that govern human existence." So in 2019, what is Mongolia's sense of itself, and how does it view its national identity? What responsibility do Mongolians feel about its future?

I have unfortunately little idea about the genetic and environmental factors that predispose a person to discard all ethical impulses. Certainly if one of today's xenophobic leaders uses inflammatory rhetoric to tell his or her followers who should not be a community member, it is a harbinger of violence, whether we speak of Nigeria or the United States. The only solution is to cease tolerating intolerance, to strive for the inclusion of all with acceptance, compassion, and kindness—and to join minds and hearts.

1994

Determined to do the survey we failed to complete last year, and especially eager to locate potential new reserves, I arrived back in UB on July 18, 1994. Kay is with me this time, which makes me happy. Word has reached me that the UNDP has a new program manager named Jan Sweetering. Full of anticipation, I go to the program office—and a wave of gloom engulfs me. All contracts, including mine, have been held up at the UNDP office in New York. Everyone is uncertain about the future. Daily allowances have been cut and the number of consultants reduced. The new manager thinks that wildlife studies and school education programs are a waste of money, and several such projects have already been terminated.

My immediate concern is to assemble a Mongolian team for our survey. I'm delighted that two former colleagues want to come. One is the argali biologist S. Amgalanbaatar (Amga). The root *baatar* in his name means "hero" in Mongolian, and he is a hero to me for his dedication to fieldwork. The other is D. Batbold from the Ministry of Nature and Environment. G. Olziimaa, a graduate botany student at the National University, is a most welcome addition. Badamkhand, the wife of the Gobi Park biologist R. Tulgat, of the National Parks Department, is appointed to join us. A man named Oyunaa, who speaks German and English, becomes our interpreter. There are also three drivers, one for a small truck that carries gasoline barrels and the others for our two jeeps. One jeep, along with Batbold and Badamkhand, will return after ten days, but the rest of us will continue on for a month. Kay is, of course, part of the team. I am pointedly asked if UNDP pays her, and I assure everyone that it does not.

We set a departure date after administrative issues have been resolved, but are told that the day is not auspicious. Finally we head off across the steppe on July 31, across the flowering landscape of gentians, asters, and bluebells. We camp near the town of Mandalgovi, our tents hidden in a fold of the hills to discourage robbers. The next afternoon we stop in Tsogt Ovoo, a county town, to collect information from the local government about the number of people and livestock, and about wildlife and tourist attractions. We realize that we need to visit all the county towns during our survey to obtain such basic information. In Dalanzadgad, the capital of Omnogovi Province, we interview Governor Mijidorj, who also provides us with a letter that enables us to buy 150 liters (39.6 gals.) of gasoline. The government depot is only allowed to sell 400 liters (about 105 gals.) per day, and these are already gone, while a long line of vehicles has lined up for tomorrow's ration. But thanks to the governor's letter we receive our gasoline. Near Dalanzadgad are large deposits of coal and various minerals such as copper, and there is oil as well. Once we stopped at an oil rig operated by SOCO, a company with headquarters in London. It's still a small operation, a mere 250 barrels a day, but more drilling sites are planned for this area. The oil rig is leased from China, the oil is trucked to China, and most workers are Chinese. I wonder how this steppe will look after several years of careless development, with excavated pits, piles of detritus, roads, industrial sprawl, and pools of toxic chemicals. Better that I just absorb the beauty of the steppe in the days ahead.

Our survey area includes fifteen counties and comprises about 57,900 square miles (150,000 km²) or nearly 10 percent of Mongolia. That's about five times the size of New Hampshire, my home state. As I saw last year, most of the region consists of rolling plains at about 3,300 feet (1,000 m) in elevation, broken at intervals by rocky ranges and hills up to 5,575 feet (1,700 m) high. The area can be broadly divided into several vegetation zones, with desert and semi-desert in the southern part near the China border. Adjoining it is a broad band of dry grass steppe, which grades into moister steppe farther north. About 95 percent of the area is rangeland, and the rest barren sand and rock. Surface water is limited to occasional springs and ephemeral pools. These are usually occupied by livestock herders, who still have to depend mostly on wells, especially during droughts.

Parched mountain ranges expand to vast plains, where small herds of black-tailed gazelle look pale and insubstantial as they seem to float away in the heat waves. Khulan (wild asses) are common too in places, singly or in herds, their tan and elegant forms blending into the landscape. We note one male as he closely follows two females, each with a young. He chases one of the females, and she, obviously annoyed, slashes at him with her hind legs. Another time, in the early morning hours, I hear khulan bray in a sandy riverbed near camp. It is a peculiar sound something like the cross between a duck's squawk and a dog's bark, ending with a growl. Then I observe the khulan at dawn pawing craters in the riverbed and drinking the water that seeps in. There are three males, and soon five females, each with a foal, arrive. One male approaches the females, groaning and with ears laid back. A female swivels around and kicks him. Another male tries to herd the females, as if wanting to collect a harem. Not interested in these crude overtures, the females leave. I suspect each male has his own territory nearby but comes to water both to drink and to assert his presence.

I note with interest the difference in behavior between the kiang (Tibetan wild ass) on the remote Tibetan Plateau and the khulan at the approach of our vehicle. The kiang would usually stand and watch us alertly or even run along parallel to us, seemingly quite curious. The khulan, by contrast, would bolt as soon as they perceived us, knowing that a hunter might inhabit the vehicle.

Counting wildlife is a cooperative venture on our trip. "Three gazelle on the right," Oyunaa may say, and we take note of two females

*A large aggregation of Mongolian gazelles shimmers
in evening light on the eastern steppe.*

and a young. "A single khulan," exclaims Olziimaa, and we each record
this in our notebooks. A flock of Pallas's sandgrouse streaks low over
the steppe in a tight flock. "How many?" I ask. Estimates range from
125 to 200. I note occasional birds in passing to myself, such as desert
wheatear and crested lark, and point out to my companions a black
kite and several kestrels riding the updrafts by a ridge.

In an area of low hills speckled with rock outcrops we come upon
a trophy-hunting camp named Modon Usnii. There are five gers, and
a Spaniard resides in one. He has just completed a nine-day hunt,
cruising around the area in a jeep while searching for prey. The salted
hides and heads of his bag are drying in the sun. There is a Gobi argali,
age eight years, his heavy, curling horns 41 inches (106 cm) long. The
Spaniard has also shot a modest-sized ibex, one black-tailed gazelle,
and one Mongolian gazelle. Between 1967 and 1989 a total of 1,630

argali were shot as trophies in Mongolia, according to Amga, for which foreign hunters paid $20,000–$30,000 for each license. Of this fee, 6 percent went to the national government, 20 percent to the hunting company, 15 percent to the province, and 5 percent to the county. The householders who live in the hunting area and could help protect the wildlife received nothing. With a new hunting law in 2000, 50 percent of such fees must be spent on conservation. The price of a trophy license was raised to $70,000–$80,000 in 2017. But how much of this do local communities receive? A hunting camp operates for a few months in summer and autumn and closes for the rest of the year, offering at that time no active wildlife and habitat protection. After all the trophy-sized animals have been shot, the hunting camp moves elsewhere. The whole system is a commercial venture of little direct benefit to wildlife or the local people. However, we did gain several good meals from our visit. The Spaniard generously presented us with one of his two gazelles, its meat tender and less fatty than that of sheep or goat.

The Martin Luther University in Germany publishes a series of volumes titled *Exploration into the Biological Resources of Mongolia.* The 2016 volume has an article on argali by several authors, one of them Amga. It notes that the argali is scattered in many small and isolated populations in Mongolia, spread over about 23,100 square miles (60,000 km²) mainly in along the curve of the Altai Mountains. Each one of these small populations is highly susceptible to extinction. In recent decades, the argali has been "declining rapidly" largely due to "poaching and competition with domestic livestock." Censuses conducted by research teams in 2009 calculated that around 5,000 argali survived in the two provinces through which we are traveling, and the total in the country was around 18,000. We had tallied 182 argali by the end of the trip, all too often just spotting their flashing white rumps as the animals fled out of sight. The good news is that the argali is extending its range and seen now occasionally in areas from which the animals have been absent for years.

Along our route we stop at the Ulgyin monastery, now mostly a maze of crumbling mud walls. The monastery once housed fifteen hundred monks and had existed for 140 years, but packs of rampaging Mongolians killed or evicted them all in 1937. Even so, the remnants sanctify the site. Now, after several decades, a new monastery is emerging, a one-room structure with six monks and a boy who live nearby. We talk to the head monk, Dambarentchin, a stocky seventy-eight-year-old, who wears a scarlet cloak with turquoise cuffs. When asked about wildlife around the monastery, he notes that khulan are increasing, ibex are scarce, and argali have never recovered after the government shot over two hundred for meat in the 1950s. I ask if the monastery could use its moral force to stop hunting in the area. Dambarentchin replies that not the local people but outsiders with guns and cars are the problem. Nearby we can see an oil derrick, a portent of the future. About 6 miles (10 km) away is a petrified forest, he also tells us, and offers his brother as a guide to show it to us. This forest is located in a narrow, barren valley. There are many standing stumps about three feet tall and almost as wide. Some fallen trees are ten feet or more long, all turned to smooth, shining stone, pale red and yellow-brown in color. It is possible to count tree rings in some. I glide my hand over these ancient trees, marveling at their persistence and wondering what strange creatures rested in their shadows. Vandals have smashed some of the stumps and carried away the pieces.

When we reach the county town of Mandakh in Dornogovi Province, the local leader urges us to head south to see the fossil sites after we mention the petrified trees. We have too little gasoline to make such a detour, but he sells us 200 liters (52.8 gals.). After consider-

*Several old monks have returned to the Gobi's Ulgyin
monastery, which was destroyed in the 1930s.*

able searching, we ask at a ger for directions. A herdsman tells us to
look for an isolated hillock with two stone cairns (oboos) on top.
Local spirits are said to dwell in an oboo, a belief that points to a pre-
Buddhist past, when shamanism was the religion. We camp at the
base of the hillock. Kay and I wander off at dawn. Scattered over the
gravel steppe are what appear to be white stones — all of them pieces
of dinosaur bone. It is a sensuous feeling to stroke the smooth bone
of an animal that lived some 60 million years ago.

Another day while strolling among some granite outcrops, I find
many quartz chips, obviously flakes discarded by Neolithic makers
of stone tools. I bring Kay to the site. She had majored in anthro-
pology in college, taken part in excavations, and never lost her interest in ancient history. We soon find a number of stone tools, among
them scrapers and broken arrowheads. Stone Age hunters had already

been here in pursuit of ibex and argali. On a boulder is a stick nest, and in it, to my delight, is a huge brown-feathered cinereous vulture, almost fledged.

We would drive for many miles each day and seldom encounter a ger. Mongolia has a population density of only about 4 persons per square mile (2.6 km²), and most of the people live in towns. The statistics we gather in county towns bear out the low human population density. There are only about 66,500 people in the two provinces we are surveying. Half of these live in the provincial capitals Dalanzadgad and Saynshand, and many others concentrate around the county towns. Excluding the capitals, the human density in various counties ranges from 0.7 to 2.9 square miles per person. The region also holds nearly one million head of livestock, mostly sheep and goats, but also horses, cattle, and camels. Large tracts have no people because of water scarcity.

Heading southeast we enter Khatanbulag County, and encounter a marvelous concentration of wildlife. On the rather desolate plain, sparsely covered with saxaul and spiny *Caragana* shrub, many black-tailed gazelle have congregated in some of the largest herds I've seen anywhere. As many as 80, mostly females with their offspring, are together, vibrantly alive. We also encounter khulan: one herd of at least 500, another of about 250, a third of 234, and some small ones. The following night a violent storm hits us for over an hour with driving rain, loud thunder, and a sky brilliant with lightning. Creeks roar with flashfloods. Did the gazelle and khulan sense the coming local rain and gather in the area, just as the wildebeest in Tanzania's Serengeti travel toward the moist air of distant storms to take advantage of the green, nutritious herbage that will soon appear?

Our route takes us east toward the Beijing-UB railroad line. Suddenly we begin to encounter Mongolian gazelles, not just a few but large herds. Ahead I note a rather barren hillside with a pinkish flush

Mongolian gazelles crowd around a seepage to drink during a period of drought.

resembling a field of flowers. But the flowers flow uphill, transforming themselves into a herd of about 2,000 Mongolian gazelles that had been bedded down. We see an estimated 6,000 gazelles that day. Of these we manage to classify 689, with males and females equal in number and half the adult females accompanied by a trailing youngster. When the railroad was built in the 1950s, the fenced track severed a main migration route of these gazelles. Their principal habitat is the eastern steppe, where their favored and most nutritious food plants are abundant, especially in winter. These include *Stipa, Agropyron,* and other grasses, various forbs, and the tips of sagebrush. Most displaced animals tend to stay near the railroad. Those that try to cross the barbed-wire fence, some to rejoin the main migration and others to gain access to the pasture along the railroad track, become entangled. A number of gazelles die slowly there, hooked and hanging on the barbed wire. Others struggle free, their hides torn. Gazelles that find a gap in the fence or otherwise manage to reach the track may then be squashed by a speeding train. Khulan distribution has also been fragmented by these railroad fences. Unable to jump over or crawl under the fences, khulan remain west of the railroad instead of expanding their range into the great eastern steppe. Over- or underpasses or modifications to the fence have been suggested for years, and in 2019 at least are being discussed.

We finally reach the town of Erdene, bordering the railroad. Our driver, Bor, and Olziimaa head to a store, where they find only soap, matches, and vodka. On their way back, sullen thugs surround Bor and demand 500 tugrik to buy vodka, and for good measure slug him in the eye. Now we drive north to Saynshand, where we hope to buy some bread. The former Russian part of town, like such sections in most other towns, is now a pile of rubble as if after a bombing raid. The five-story apartment buildings are empty shells, the power plant has been burned, and only the walls remain of the community hall, all destroyed in 1990 and 1991 as soon as the Russians left. But a statue of Lenin still stands, though the hands are broken off and the face is smashed.

It is time to return to UB, and we arrive there on August 30, having driven about 2,300 miles (3,700 km), as well as walked many hours over the landscape. It has been a splendid trip, with a congenial, interested, and hardworking team, everyone contributing to camp work and wildlife observations. We summarize our wildlife data from the two provinces. Sometimes we could not count the number of animals in a herd because of their shyness. And, of course, it is easier to spot wildlife on the plains than in the rough terrain where we did few surveys. This gave us a small number of sightings of argali and ibex. Our tally is 39 ibex, including a herd of 18 males; 182 argali; 1,062 black-tailed gazelle; 1,310 khulan; and over 6,000 Mongolian gazelle. This information was all presented in a detailed report to UNDP and the Mongolian government departments concerned.

We also suggest several areas for potential reserves, and we are deeply honored and grateful that these were seriously considered and later implemented. Our suggestions were timely. Concerned about the protection of its beautiful but rapidly deteriorating landscape, the Mongolian government was receptive to proposals such as ours. Because of its abundant wildlife, we recommended that a large area along the China border be protected. It was subsequently established as the Small Gobi Strictly Protected Area in two parts, totaling 7,102 square miles (18,400 km²) in size. Just to the north is an ecological gradient from semi-desert to steppe, an ancient land with petrified trees, Neolithic stone tool and dinosaur sites, and the Ulgyin monastery. This area became a nature reserve 235 square miles (609 km²) in size. Farther to the north among granite outcrops is a place called Ikh Nart, where the argali will, I hope, now be safe from poachers and trophy hunters. It has also been designated as a nature reserve, one of 169 square miles (437 km²). By 2000, Mongolia had forty-eight protected areas covering 13 percent of the land, and it continues to add more.

Our work with the UNDP and the government in 1993 and 1994 has come to a most satisfying conclusion, benefiting the wildlife and natural habitats of Mongolia. The country, fortunately, keeps its conservation options open, as we saw on these journeys. Nature needs constant devotion and care to survive, and in the years ahead Mongolia will, we hope, take the correct paths of possibility. After all, for hundreds of years its nomadic society focused on living in harmony with nature based on the influence of Shamanism and Lamaism, which offered guidelines for the sustainable use of water, grassland, soil, and forest. A Mongolian saying, one that must never be ignored by any nomadic herder anywhere in the world, advises, "To stay in one place a long time will destroy it, but to move from one place to another after a short time will preserve it."

5

Slaughter on the Steppe

Be kind to all creatures; this is the true religion.

Gautama Buddha

Do not set up living creatures as a target.

Prophet Muhammad

Mongolia's environment is increasingly under stress as new roads penetrate pristine areas, huge coal and copper mines scar the land, oil rigs like trees grow from the steppe, and outsiders view the country as an opportunity for plunder and profit. Will Mongolians lose the collective memory of great Mongolian gazelle herds, just as Americans can no longer remember the vast herds of bison and sky-darkening flocks of passenger pigeons that have vanished into the past in the United States? When I first came to Mongolia, magnificent red deer wandered companionably around the parks of Ulaan Baatar during the winter, a more benign habitat than the deep snow in the nearby hills. They were soon gone, killed for meat and for the antlers and penises exported to China because these are thought to have medicinal use. How many residents of UB know of or remember these deer?

Wildlife has declined in recent decades throughout Mongolia, a reckless pillage by slayers of beauty that I occasionally witnessed. Since wildlife populations have not been accurately monitored, and protective laws have been only casually enforced, it is unfortunately not known how many animals of each species have been killed, legally and otherwise, or how many there once were. Local people hunt for subsistence, and the meat of gazelles has been exported for profit, as have the hides of wolf, lynx, Corsac and red fox, marmot, and various others. This alone has accounted for some two million or more animals each year. Wolf tongue, bear gall bladder, snow leopard bone, and saiga antelope horn are in demand in China for medicinal purposes, and foreign trophy hunters kill argali sheep, red deer, and others to decorate their private mortuaries.

To illustrate the decline of certain wild species, I shall briefly describe the killing of Mongolian or white-tailed gazelles and Siberian marmots and the capture of saker falcons. The actual numbers I quote merely give an indication, an order of magnitude, of the animals killed. Precise records were usually not kept; illegal kills are difficult to measure; and some records are withheld from the public by the government. Valuable sources of information can be found in the reference list, especially Katie Scharf and her coauthors, "Herders and Hunters in a Transitional Economy," James Wingard and Peter Zahler, *Silent Steppe,* and Kirk A. Olson, "Ecology and Conservation of Mongolian Gazelle."

Mongolian Gazelles

I see them crowded side by side and row upon row like regiments on parade in the yellow autumn grass of the steppe. They are on their bellies, tan hides toward the sky, and white rumps touching. They have been gutted and their lower legs have been hacked off. A pile of bloody heads, both male and female, lies off to one side. About four thousand Mongolian gazelle have been mass slaughtered, some illegally inside a reserve, the meat and hides destined for export to China.

But lying in the hot sun waiting for transport, the carcasses begin to rot. The Chinese refuse to accept the rotting meat, and instead it is sold cheaply in local markets. On another occasion, a total of eighteen thousand gazelles were slaughtered for export with lead bullets from automatic weapons. Hungary and Austria refused to accept the bodies because, it was claimed, the lead content of the meat was too high for safe consumption. Again the meat was sold locally and the hides wasted. When I mentioned such carelessness and waste to the governor of Dornod Province, where many such "hunts" are held, he merely replied, "We must have benefit from the gazelles."

Between 1932 and 1976 a total of about 845,000 gazelles were recorded as having been killed in Mongolia for the trade with Russia. An additional 100,000 to 150,000 gazelles were shot during the war years of 1939–1945 to feed Russian troops. Commercial hunts between 1980 and 1992 accounted for 247,108 more gazelles, with a range of zero in 1989 and 1990 to 34,800 in 1987. The meat went mostly to European countries and China, and the viscera were sent to Russia to feed sable and other species on fur farms. Some gazelles migrate north into Russia and south into China. "When gazelle go to Russia," a county leader told me, "they don't come back." However, they seem to be safe in the Sokhondinsky Nature Reserve of Zabaikalsky Province, where about 6,500 have been counted. In China, an estimated 2.5 million Mongolian gazelles were killed between 1956 and 1966. Today the species occurs in China only in a narrow strip along the Mongolian border of the Inner Mongolia Autonomous Region. Gazelle populations there are difficult to assess because many animals move out of Mongolia to China for the winter, from October to late February, and then return north. Their travels take them past Mongolian and Chinese border posts, where guards shoot them to supplement their own meager food rations. The Mongolian military is reported to have shot 30,000 gazelles in 1985. Xiaoming Wang, a Chinese wildlife biologist and former colleague of mine, and his colleagues surveyed gazelles in that area during the 1994–1995 winter and estimated that as many as 250,000 were present at that time.

Official hunts, even if they are inefficient and quotas are based on intuition rather than the known size of the population, still account for only a fraction of the annual death toll. Many gazelle may die during severe winters, such as the *dzud* (blizzards) of 1977 and 2009. A variety of diseases can devastate a population. About 100,000 gazelle died in 1974–1975 from what may have been foot-and-mouth disease. Foot rot, a bacterial disease we witnessed in 1998, killed thousands. And nonhuman predators, from wolves to steppe eagles, take a small percentage. Subsistence hunting by Mongolians kills a large but unknown number of gazelles annually. In Soviet times, before 1990, there were about 30,000 licensed guns, but by 2007 the number had increased to 240,000. Interviews with herder households revealed that over half of them hunt gazelles, mostly for food. In 2004 there were 40,000 licensed hunters, who killed an average of 5.2 gazelles each, or a total of about 208,000 animals. Concerned about such figures, the government banned commercial hunting for export in 2001. However, *aimak* (provincial) governments could still provide licenses to households for one gazelle each. Yet in spite of the commercial ban and great reduction in the legal harvest, China managed to import 100 tons of gazelle meat from Mongolia in 2001, the equivalent of about 6,600 animals. Empty oil tankers, trucks, and trains all are said to haul illegal gazelle bodies and other wildlife products across the border into China.

Poaching is often a direct or indirect way to make money. Monitoring our radio-collared gazelle at night on the steppe, I would note jeeps cruising around on a hunt, and I would then see such jeeps coming to Choibalsan loaded with gazelles to sell in town, where the police clearly offered impunity. Katie Scharf and her co-workers interviewed 350 households in Choibalsan and found that each consumed on average 56 pounds (25.4 kg) of gazelle meat per year, roughly the equivalent of two gazelles. This translates to about 16,000 dead gazelles in this city alone. Over a third of the households hunted for their meat.

Each *sum,* or county, has a designated government wildlife inspector, but under the difficult conditions of the 1990s the inspectors lacked vehicles and fuel, making it extremely difficult to prevent poaching and enforce laws. The illegal slaughter was at that time estimated to be at least 100,000 gazelles each year. In an important initiative, the UNDP-GEF Eastern Steppe Biodiversity Project held workshops in 2000 to train wildlife inspectors and rangers of protected areas in collecting biological data, monitoring wildlife, patrolling, and other basic management needs.

The sheep, goats, cattle, horses, and camels represent food security to a herder household, as well as potential income from their sale for essential supplies. Goat cashmere is the second-largest source of income. Hunting, of course, reduces the need for a family to eat or sell its livestock, since they can subsist on gazelle meat instead. One gazelle sells for the equivalent of five or six dollars, whereas a sheep is worth more than twenty-five dollars. In his interviews of 156 households, Kirk Olson found that those who do not hunt have considerably more domestic animals than those who do, an average of 371 to 194. Hunting also boosts a family's meager annual income, which in 2004 averaged twelve hundred dollars. At the time, a marmot hide sold for about four dollars, a red fox pelt for thirteen dollars, and a wolf skin for thirty dollars. Killing wolves was also popular as a way to reduce livestock predation. About a third of the families interviewed by Kirk had predation losses, averaging 3.7 sheep and goats annually, along with an occasional horse or cow. Even adding in the profits from hunting, a poor herder family increased its annual income by only around 10 percent.

Given such unrestrained slaughter, it is hardly surprising that there has been a drastic decrease in gazelle numbers. The species once occurred over about half of Mongolia, but during the past five or six decades its range has contracted by at least 50 percent and perhaps by as much as 75 percent. How many gazelles inhabited this region in the past? We cannot answer that, given the lack of effort to monitor and count them. It was thought that there were over a million gazelles in the 1940s but that only 250,000 to 270,000 remained by the late 1970s. Disease and drought may have reduced that number further by the early 1980s. The estimate for the following years rebounded to 300,000 to 400,000. An aerial survey over most of the range of gazelles in 1994 raised that number to a disputed 2.67 million. Kirk Olson began his detailed research on Mongolian gazelles in 1999. From 2000 to 2002 he made an intensive effort to count the gazelles by driving transects across the eastern steppe, covering an area of 30,880 square miles (80,000 km²) and counting all animals within his view. He had selected the major areas where gazelles concentrate seasonally in Dornod and Sukhbaatar Provinces. His result: an estimated 800,000 to 900,000 gazelles could be found in that area, and just over a million in the country as a whole.

In October 2003, an international workshop on gazelle management, which I attended, was held in Ulaan Baatar. Also invited was Paul Hopwood, a biologist from Australia, who informed us about that country's excellent system of harvesting and managing kangaroos. It was hoped that some of the principles could also be applied to gazelles. One product of the workshop was a report Peter Zahler and his colleagues published in a 2003 issue of the *Mongolian Journal of Biological Sciences,* "Management of Mongolian Gazelles as a Sustainable Resource." Here is the abstract:

The major output from this workshop was the general agreement that no commercial hunt can be recommended at this time. This is because of the high level of poaching that is appearing to be having a negative impact on gazelle numbers. Best estimates put the existing gazelle population at about one million and decreasing. Models have suggested that this population could sustain an annual 6% commercial offtake. However, it is estimated that the illegal offtake may be near or exceed 10% annually. If so, this would explain why the population of gazelles is decreasing even without a legal commercial hunt. While there are adequate laws to deal with poaching, there is extremely poor enforcement due to lack of funding, equipment, and will. We recommend against a commercial harvest until poaching is controlled and there is a sound monitoring system in place, and until monitoring shows gazelle populations to be stable or increasing.

Siberian Marmots

As I walked or drove across the great steppe during the early 1990s, I occasionally met a marmot sitting bolt upright, intently watching my approach. Then, judging me to be potentially dangerous, it would give a shrill whistle to alert the others and dive into its burrow. I found these large brownish and black rodents delightful and companionable members of the steppe community. But in later years, I saw marmots less and less often. Instead I came across hunters splayed on the ground waiting motionless with their rifles trained on marmot colonies. When a marmot emerges from its burrow, only a headshot will prevent it from struggling back underground to die there a slow and painful death. Sometimes I would meet a hunter with three or more dead *tarvag,* as the marmot is locally called, draped over his motorcycle. Toward the end of the decade, I mainly noted burrows that had no fresh diggings around the entrance, empty now except as refuges for spiders and crickets. A survey by J. Batbold of the eastern provinces—Dornod, Khenti, and Sukhbaatar—a region once boasting high marmot densities, revealed that only 5 percent of the existing burrows remained active; their former occupants were dead.

Marmots were once distributed over much of Mongolia, except in the desert region. They are estimated to have declined by three-quarters in recent decades for the usual reasons: the failure of meaningful legislation to protect them, lack of monitoring of their habitats, and lax enforcement of poaching laws. A major reason for the slaughter is the marmot's thick fur. Between 1920 and 1991 marmot skins were principally exported to Russia, at an average rate of about 1.2 million skins per year; a record 2,493,180 were exported in 1947. Given the large illegal trade, then as now, this figure is merely a suggestion of magnitude. Detailed official figures after 1991 are unavailable. However, in 2001 two Chinese companies in Inner Mongolia applied for a license to import 1.3 million marmot skins from Mongolia.

According to law, the marmot hunting season is from August 10 to October 15, and a hunter must buy a license, which allows him to kill three marmots. There are at least 125,000 licensed hunters. But the real and unsustainable impact of the marmot kill can be judged by some figures from the illegal hunt.

Between 1998 and 2000, Chinese customs at the Ehrenhot border post in Inner Mongolia confiscated 38,605 marmot skins, and the Manzhouli and Hohhot customs offices in Inner Mongolia recorded

*A Kazakh holds his trained golden eagle used to hunt
foxes, marmots, and other species for pelts and meat.*

166,000 illegal skins between 1999 and 2001. Also seized between
1997 and 2000 were 12,228 pounds (5,558 kg) of red deer antler and
392 pounds (178 kg) of saiga antelope horn.

Katie Scharf and her colleagues conducted market surveys and
found that "by the end of the 2001–2002 hunting season, the total
number of marmot skins observed in the eastern provincial center
markets was almost three times the quota, and four times the licensed
amount." Choibalsan, for example, declared a quota of 11,500 skins,
whereas the observed total was 42,435 skins.

The marmot hunting season was officially closed in 2005 and
2006. Even with the ban in place, hunting continued, and before
the end of August 2006 the Border Defense Agency had confiscated
26,000 skins that were headed into China.

Given the extensive legal and illegal hunting, it is unsurprising

*A marmot hunter on the eastern steppe with fresh
marmot pelts draped on his motorcycle.*

that there is a "Mongolian marmot crisis," as Susan Townsend and
Peter Zahler phrased it. They conducted extensive daytime line transects in June and July 2005 across the eastern steppe to tally used and
unused marmot burrows. They also counted the marmots themselves.
The results revealed a marmot density of about 0.12 animals per km²
(0.05 per sq. mile) as compared to a density of 50 or more in the same
region by a Mongolian team in 1990. Although the two survey methods may not be directly comparable, they nonetheless indicate that
the decline in marmots has been drastic.

Marmots are hunted for more than their hides. The meat is de-
licious and is considered a tonic for colds, asthma, and general well-
being. The sale of meat also supplements the steppe dwellers' meager
household income. Marmot fat is widely used medicinally for treat-
ment of burns, frostbite, tuberculosis, anemia, and other ailments. Yet

the marmot is not simply a species that humans find useful; it is also an important member of the complex ecological steppe community. Its disappearance from many areas of the region is no doubt harming various species which directly and indirectly depend on its presence. By digging burrows, marmots bring mineral-rich earth to the surface, and this also helps the soil absorb moisture, both processes aiding plant growth. Marmot feces above and below ground add nutrients to the soil as well. Abandoned burrows offer homes to pikas (a small cousin of the rabbit), steppe polecats, lizards, a variety of insects, and others. And the marmots themselves provide meals for a number of carnivorous species, from wolves to golden eagles, which each in its own way also affects the steppe community. There is ecological unity in diversity. Nature is a circle, from grass to marmot to lynx, that must not be broken.

Saker Falcons

The saker is the largest falcon in Central Asia, with a wingspread of up to 50 inches (127 cm). An elegant bird with a rust-brown back and heavily streaked undersides, it is also powerful, agile, and fast, making it a favorite of falconers. The bird breeds in Central Asia and winters in Iran, Pakistan, and other southern areas. It is a special favorite of hunters from Saudi Arabia and the United Arab Emirates. In the early 1970s, our family lived in Pakistan. I remember hearing news of Arabs arriving in large private planes, most of the seats occupied by falcons. They had come to hunt the rare houbara bustard, a large terrestrial bird found in the desert, and this they did almost to the bird's extinction. Saker falcons are most easily obtained from China and Mongolia. Mongolia exported 446 falcons to the Arab countries between 1994 and 1999 for a fee of $2,750 per bird. This price was subsequently raised, as noted in a newspaper article in the

Mongol Messenger dated August 1, 2001: "The new prices are $4500 per falcon plus an export fee and customs duties. . . . The limit this year for falconers is 150." China also instituted export fees of up to $2,500 per bird. Naturally these prices stimulated the smuggling of saker falcons. Between 1993 and 1997 there were thirty cases of attempted smuggling at the Beijing airport, which included 450 falcons. China's State Forestry Administration confiscated about 1,000 saker falcons between 1992 and 1995, whereas Mongolia confiscated only 69 falcons between 1993 and 1999. The municipal government of Abu Dhabi, the capital of the United Arab Emirates, instituted a program to raise saker falcons, as well as other falcon species such as the peregrine and gyrfalcon, even though captive reared and trained birds tend to be less adept hunters than wild-caught adults. By 1999, according to Peter Gwin's article in *National Geographic,* Abu Dhabi's breeding station was said to house several thousand falcons, an indication of both the initial plunder of these birds from the wild and the demand for falcons. The city did at least institute strict import regulations for falcons. But the capture of falcons in Mongolia continued with government approval. At least 184 were exported in 2001. By September 2002 a total of 205 had been exported that year, of which 110 went to Kuwait, 45 to Saudi Arabia, 10 to Qatar, and 40 to Syria.

While driving across Mongolia's treeless steppe, I occasionally spotted a saker falcon nest on the ground composed of a few sticks, vulnerable to any fox, human, or other predator. One nest, however, was on the roof of a defunct and abandoned tractor. When I found it in 2001, it had four young, their feathers partially grown. I checked on the nest occasionally, but on July 14 the young were gone. The nest had been robbed by poachers, as fresh car tracks revealed. The two adult falcons still lingered nearby. Damn the poachers: they could have left one young for the parents. And damn the falconers who thoughtlessly were depleting a natural treasure for their mere amusement.

Mongolia has had an ever-changing series of hunting laws since it achieved independence in 1920. The first laws of that decade gave protection to animals in the breeding season and established a system of hunting licenses and fees. The annihilation of wolves was encouraged. As Mongolia was increasingly drawn into the Soviet system, its wildlife trade had by the 1950s shifted wholly away from China and other countries. Herders were then concentrated in collectives under full government control. The Society of Hunters was established in 1956. Six years later it was transferred to the Ministry of Agriculture, where it was administered by the Central Hunting Association. It had a branch in each county that regulated all hunting and enforcement activities.

As relations between the Soviet Union and China improved in the 1970s, the wildlife trade between Mongolia and China resumed. In 1981, Mongolia's parliament mandated that censuses of forests and fish, bird, and mammal species be conducted. At that time about 5 percent of the country's foreign earnings came mainly from the sale of furs. But just as conservation efforts began to stabilize, everything collapsed in 1989, when the Soviet Union withdrew and Mongolia's economy crashed, causing inflation, unemployment, and poverty. A new Law of Hunting in 1995 stipulated fees and licenses for various activities related to wildlife. Rare species were placed under the jurisdiction of the Ministry of Nature and Environment. All other species were to be protected and managed by the counties rather than the central government, an unfortunate delegation of authority that has created many problems. In 2000 a modified Law of Fauna was passed. One of its stipulations was that the penalty for killing an endangered species would be twice the economic value of the animal, as determined by the central government. A snow leopard's value has been set at $450. That is perhaps a third to a half of a herder's annual cash income.

I have provided these data to offer a brief historical perspective by which past and present can be compared. Greed and indifference to long-term sustainability of the wildlife populations have resulted in drastic declines of species. Yet in spite of decades of wildlife misman-agement, the remnants are large enough to enable them to recover. And, above all, Mongolians retain some concern for their environ-ment. Even during its recent period of greatest difficulties, Mongolia established many new protected areas. In 1991 there were eleven such areas covering 21,615 square miles (55,983 km^2) or 3.6 percent of the country. By 2006 there were fifty-six protected areas covering 79,248 square miles (205,306 km^2), 13.5 percent of the country. The goal is to protect 30 percent by 2030. When these laws were passed, the coun-try had neither funds nor staff to protect and manage the areas. For instance, the Mongolia Protected Area Administration in the eastern part of the country had in 1994 a staff of fifteen, of which eleven sat in the Choibalsan office. They owned two vehicles, three motorcycles, and one horse for transport, and had only four guards to protect and manage the vast steppes which even then were considered the next frontier for agricultural and industrial development.

6

Nomrog

Ethics in its unqualified form extends responsibility to everything that has life.

Albert Schweitzer

The superior man seeks what is right; the inferior one what is profitable.

Confucius

The great eastern steppe remains in my mind and heart as I first saw it in 1989. It extends to the horizon, with few people, many Mongolian gazelles, and little development, its ecological integrity intact. A number of protected areas have since been established to offer the plants and animals there a future. Among these is the Nomrog Strictly Protected Area (SPA) at the far eastern tip of the region adjoining China. Although it was established almost thirty years ago, in 1992, it is so remote that almost no one has heard of it. Such a peaceful and bucolic landscape seems to irritate development agencies with hundreds of million of dollars to spend. They insist that there must be a need to "reduce poverty," "improve quality of life," and create "economic and development impact" through "sustainable growth."

The eastern steppe became part of a Regional Environmental Protection Plan for Inner Mongolia and Mongolia in an initiative funded by the Asian Development Bank (ADB). The bank contracted the planning to the Transportation and Economic Research Association (TERA), a consultancy based in the United States with an office in Beijing. The association's proposed plan naturally stressed "infrastructure development," as that is always a good way for a company to make money. A special focus of the plan was the Nomrog SPA. It extends over a mere 1,201 square miles (3,112 km²), yet TERA proposed implementing a major tourist development program there.

The Mongolian government and its various advisers had proposed constructing a so-called Millennium Highway from UB across the middle of the steppe and right through the Nomrog SPA into China as a major commercial connection between the two countries. They are also considering adding a railroad. Such developments would, of course, disrupt the steppe yet again with fences and other obstruction and hinder the gazelle migrations.

The Millennium Highway was planned without forethought. It bypasses Choibalsan, a major commercial center, and runs through the center of the steppe instead of eastward near the China border; it also goes directly through the Nomrog SPA, instead of heading north and east into China. Of immediate concern to Kirk Olson and myself in 2002 were the development plans for Nomrog. A paved "environmentally friendly feeder road" is to penetrate the protected area, including a bridge over a major river. If a road cuts through a wilderness area, it provides easy access to poachers and promotes unregulated tourist and other development. The ADB prides itself on "preventing environmental degradation." The TERA plan almost taunts the ADB by proposing to add a zoo and botanical garden to Nomrog. Because such development in a Strictly Protected Area is illegal under Mongolian law, TERA suggested eliminating part of the protected area to make development there legal!

Kirk and I wanted to evaluate the Nomrog situation by checking out the tourist potential and making a wildlife survey, and we did so for a week in September 2002. Nomrog has a special interest to us because of the unique Manchurian plant and animal species it holds that are found nowhere else in Mongolia. The area represents the most southern part of the Great Khinghan Mountains, which extend north into the Manchurian part of China.

I flew to Choibalsan to meet Kirk, who now has an apartment there to be near the steppe and his gazelle studies. I also meet his co-worker, Daria Odonkhuu. I had worked in the field with Daria and found him to be a delightful and hardworking companion. Kirk is now part of the UNDP-GEF multimillion-dollar Eastern Steppe Bio-diversity Project. It has an office here in town with a staff of seven, and an additional four staff members are in the field. The objectives of the project include strengthening management of protected areas and incorporating conservation into development plans. Until now the appalling development plans for Nomrog do not seem to have been of urgent concern.

We receive two disturbing news items. The governor of Dornod Province in the far eastern steppe has apparently given a Chinese company in Inner Mongolia permission to harvest hay from about 49,400 acres (20,000 ha) and export it to China. A road is being built into the area—by imported Chinese laborers, rather than unemployed Mongolians. Furthermore, part of the hay cutting will be inside the Mongol-Dornod Strictly Protected Area. Many objections have been raised to this plan, in part because the hay might be needed locally during a drought or severe winter.

I also learn that the current minister of the environment, Ulam-bayar Barsbold, has given a Japanese company, GICA, permission to export wolf hides to Japan for fur coats. I hope word reaches the wolf packs to be extra careful.

Seed heads of feather grass glint yellow in the sun as on September 10, 2002, we head east on a road that traces the China border. At a border post we ask a Mongolian guard if we may look at the border fence to see if wildlife are able to travel back and forth between the two countries, and he takes us. The Mongolian fence has collapsed. Not far beyond is a simple Chinese wire fence and then a fence with twelve strands of barbed wire, six feet high. But every mile or so is an open gate through which cars and gazelles can travel.

After some hours, we approach a large lake, the Buyr Nuur. A river flows into it flanked by tall willow shrubs. Cormorants in long lines streak like arrows across the sky. We set up our tents on a low bluff above the river. Around 7:00 several wolves howl; I hear them again shortly after midnight. Nature here remains more or less intact, and I contentedly go back to sleep.

Our route veers southeast toward the county town of Sumber, also called Halhgol. Near our track, on the grass slope of a low hill, is a reclining Buddha made of rocks. He is about sixty feet tall and lies on his back. He was buried during the Great Terror in the 1930s, and has recently been excavated and repaired with cement. Circling the site are rock slabs with carved Buddha figures, some standing, some pushed over and broken. Near Sumber stand tall spires with wings and a star mounted on top. Rusting tanks on pedestals commemorate a major battle in the summer of 1939 when a combined Mongolian and Russian army repulsed the invading Japanese. We spot two raccoon dogs, a species native to the Far East, the first I have ever seen. With their black face masks and ringed tails they somewhat resemble the American raccoon, but their long coats give them a disheveled appearance. They scurry away. Kirk and I follow slowly on foot, and they suddenly vanish. They have crouched motionless, only to flee once more when we draw closer.

We reach Sumber, a town of sixteen hundred people, after a drive of 205 miles (330 km) from Choibalsan. There we meet our guide, wildlife ranger L. Myagmasuren, a middle-aged, pleasant man who will take us to the Nomrog SPA, some 80 miles (130 km) distant. As we approach the reserve through the buffer zone, I see not hills and valleys covered with boreal forest, as I had expected, but broad expanses of grassland with occasional stands of birch and aspen. Willows border a river below. Only about 20 percent of the protected area is covered by forest, I'm informed, including stands of planted pine. The tawny grass hills and the forest patches with leaves in autumn gold stretch before us without sign of human presence. I scan the terrain for wildlife and note that a number of forest patches have been partly or wholly burned in recent years, the bare trunks still standing. Wildfires sweeping through the tall grasslands over the years have been largely responsible for the treeless hills and valleys. And the tall, dry grasses just seem to be waiting for a spark. There are said to be brown bear, red deer, and moose here, but the only wildlife I see is a flock of about twenty Daurian partridges which erupts near us with a clatter of wings. At 6:30 we reach the guard post, consisting of several small white buildings in a valley. After checking in with a guard, we set up camp on a nearby bluff overlooking the Halchin River.

The night temperature is below freezing. At dawn we climb the hill behind camp through frost-covered grass to greet the warming sun. A fogbank traces the river, and the grassland glistens. We pack up camp and head east. It's only about 15 miles (24 km) to our next campsite, but our progress is slow because the track is unusually bumpy. When I get out of the car to relieve the ache in my back, I discover the reason. Hidden in the grass are endless mounds of dirt about a foot high, some old and some new. These are made by a subterranean gray-brown rodent, the Manchurian zokor. More satisfying, we see two roe deer fleetingly, a rust-brown male with tiny antlers and a gray female. They are about the size of a domestic goat but are slim and sleek. Later I hear a roe deer give its repeated alarm call, a hoarse roaring bark that alerts the neighborhood to potential danger.

Odonkhuu and I go for a stroll in the afternoon. Walking is not easy here; the trail is a real ankle-twister. There are the zokor mounds hidden in the grass, patches of tussock, occasional mudholes, cracks in the soil, and spiny plants, among other hazards. In a stand of burned birch we take note of waist-high saplings, a sign of the forest trying to survive. A black chicken-sized bird with white on its wings, a black grouse, flushes before us. We see no other wildlife of note, but Kirk and Myagmasuren recorded two lone red deer males on their walk, one of them bugling to announce the rut.

While shifting camp once again, we stop on a ridge overlooking a wide valley to admire the view. Kirk exclaims a single word, "Moose." There below are four moose, a male, two females, and a yearling, two of them lying down. The antlers of the male draw my immediate attention. Unlike the moose I'm familiar with in North America, with their broad, palmate antlers, this male, characteristic of Manchurian moose, has antlers with three short tines each, more like a typical deer. We camp nearby.

The next morning, September 17, Kirk and I leave early to explore the forests and ridges. Six black grouse flush, startling us with their whirr of wings. We note where wild pigs have rooted in the soil. And then we hear wolves howl near the river and descend the slope toward their music. I quote from my field notes: "Two grey-brown wolves flee, looking over their shoulder back at us. Then a large pup, two-thirds the size of the adults, trots from nearby willows, meanders around, and turns in our direction. Below, in the grass by a couple of small willows, is a trampled area, apparently a kill site. The pup sniffs and picks up a wad of skin. It chews a bit, then carries the skin into the willows and leaves it there. Briefly it returns. A second pup appears, bone in mouth, spots us and flees." We have been observing the wolves for half an hour. Now we examine where they have been. A roe deer has been killed—blood and rumen are visible, as well as some intestine and backbone, and nearby a shoulder blade. We look for but cannot find the head. By a cliff in the vicinity is the frame of an old poachers' camp. Inside we find a red deer skull with shed antlers. A bullet hole pierces the pedicel, and inside the skull is a flattened bullet. The hole is partly overgrown, so the deer did not die immediately. Our guide says the bullet is from a Russian Kalashnikov. Mongolian border guards here carry such a weapon.

It is September 18 and time to head back to UB. Our tally of large ungulates is twenty-seven roe deer, eleven moose, and three red deer, the last-named probably especially scarce because its large antlers and penis are widely used in Chinese traditional medicines. The brown bear is rare—we noted only one old digging—because its gall bladder and other body parts are also prized in medicine, and its cooked paws are a special delicacy at official Chinese banquets. We stop to report our findings to the head of the guard post, a phlegmatic individual without much interest in Nomrog. But he does tell us that the border guards recently apprehended three North Koreans. They were transferred to the South Korean embassy in UB and sent on to South Korea. The town of Sumber is apparently a transit point for fleeing North Koreans. How do such refugees manage to traverse some six hundred miles (965 km) through two Chinese provinces to reach Mongolia?

I was happy with our visit to the wilderness of Nomrog, and I know that it must endure. Problems, as stated in our report, abound: the "evidence of poaching, lack of a permanent presence of a park warden inside the reserve, the poorly patrolled border with China, and anecdotal evidence that border guards promote hunting and fishing within the protected area indicate that there is a lack of serious commitment to preserve the area." If illegal hunting were controlled, the wildlife would surely increase. Small-scale tourism—hiking and horseback riding among moose and roe deer with perhaps a distant wolf howl—would not be overly invasive, and tourists would be entranced by this peaceful and benign landscape. As to the dismal TERA development plan, Kirk and I wrote a strong ten-page critique of it and sent it to the Asian Development Bank, TERA, and different departments of the Mongolian government at the state and provincial levels in October 2002. In that report we state bluntly that "we object vigorously to that plan for economic, ethical, aesthetic, and biological reasons."

As always, I try to remain aware of subsequent changes in an area even if I am not directly involved with it anymore. By 2017 there have indeed been various changes in Nomrog. The protected area has survived, though it continues to be under development pressure. Myagmasuren, who was our 2002 guide, is now the director of a local museum. The reserve has an ineffective director, it's being said, with the result that the rangers "lack discipline and desire to be in the field." The buffer zone, uninhabited when we were there, now has two mining operations and a third under construction. Although the Millennial Highway has not yet been built, a road has been put in and a proposed bridge to which we had objected was built a few years ago, ultimately giving direct access to China for the export of mining products. Widespread hay cutting and some wheat farming also occur in the buffer zone. Indeed, there was an attempt to open 5,000 square kilometers (1,930 sq. miles) for intensive farming, but this proposal is on hold. I've also been told that "almost all of the non-forested areas surrounding Nomrog on the Chinese side have been extensively modified."

Mongolia has many ancient rules and guidelines that once shaped attitudes toward the environment based on the knowledge that if people take care of the natural world it will take care of them. With respect to mineral and oil extraction, one rule states that underground treasures must never be removed, and a second emphasizes that foreigners must never be informed about such treasures. These principles seem to have been discarded in Nomrog and elsewhere in the country. Will Mongolians some day return to their basic traditional values of respect for the land?

7

Among Mongolian Gazelles

The continued survival of Mongolia's large ungulate populations will depend on whether Mongolia's economic development proceeds at the expense of its natural heritage or whether development will be successfully integrated with biodiversity and ecosystem conservation goals.

> *Nyamsuren Batsaikhan et al., "Conserving the World's Finest Grassland Amidst Ambitious National Development" (2014)*

I wish to speak a word for Nature, for absolute freedom and wilderness.

> *Henry David Thoreau*

My favorite area in Mongolia is the great eastern steppe that had as yet been little modified by humankind when I first visited it in 1989. At about 96,500 square miles (250,000 km²), roughly the size of the United Kingdom or Italy, it was the largest pristine grassland remaining in the world. Here one can travel toward a distant horizon and see only waves of grass leaning with the wind. And it hosts Mongolian gazelles, about a million of them, the largest wildlife concentration remaining in Asia. The gazelles flow across the landscape, a tawny flood of animals, a sublime wonder of nature, the air vibrating to the yips and bleats by which mothers and young retain con-

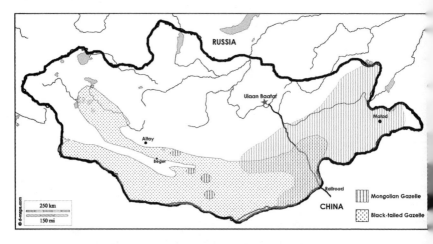

The distribution of Mongolian gazelle and black-tailed gazelle in Mongolia.

tact. Where are they going and why are they constantly on the move, here one day and gone the next? The best time to obtain preliminary answers to questions such as these is during the gazelle's birth season, from late June to early July. I went to Mongolia at that time of year in 1998, 1999, and 2000 and collaborated with gazelle biologists Badamjavin Lhagvasuren (Lhagva), Kirk Olson, Daria Odonkhuu, and others in studying these animals. Of my months in Mongolia, I have spent more time with gazelles than with any other species because they offer so much joy and also insight into their lives.

Having witnessed the migration of caribou in Arctic Alaska, wildebeest in the Serengeti of Tanzania, and Tibetan antelope or chiru on the Tibetan Plateau of China, I treasure my magic moments with the great herds. On one occasion, Lhagva and I stood on a hill at dusk. Gazelles crowded the plain, the sun's last rays transforming them into tiny, glinting points of light that moved on into shadowed hills. I strive to protect such memories and the animals which offer them.

June–July 1998, November 1998

I arrived at UB on June 8, 1998, and Lhagva met me at the airport. Afterward, I make the rounds of old friends such as Jachliin Tserendeleg. At the United Nations Development Programme office, which handles the Eastern Steppe Biodiversity Project, I meet Altangeral Enkhbat, the new coordinator. There, too, is Andrew Laurie, just arrived to spend three years in Choibalsan on the steppe project. Andrew and I had first met in the Serengeti in the late 1960s when he came to assist with projects. In 1972 we studied Persian wild goats together in Pakistan. Richard Reading, Mark Johnstad, and others have also remained as part of the ever-increasing foreign contingent. We have occasional dinners at a restaurant named Douala, managed by a woman from Cameroon. Pizzas, not just boiled mutton and cabbage, are available, and shops have a variety of goods, even bananas from China. UB is slowly becoming cosmopolitan.

We leave for Choibalsan on June 12. Our team is small. A man named Chuluun, who claims to be a driver, is behind the wheel. The rest of the team consists of Lhagva, his wife, Attan Suvd, who will be our cook, and me. At first we make our way on a stretch of good highway built by the Japanese, but it comes to an abrupt end, and we are back on a typical steppe road, parallel ruts churning through sand and soil. The dun landscape becomes green as we continue east. Pairs of demoiselle cranes leap in courtship. Mongolian larks flash their black-and-white wings as they flush when our vehicle passes. A red fox peers at us from behind a shrub. When a black storm cloud looms ahead, we decide to camp and quickly set up our tents. Suvd cooks a beef-potato-carrot stew. Two teenage boys on horseback stop by. We have not seen a gazelle all day and ask the boys if they know where we might find them. "Perhaps up in the hills eating wild onions," replies one. It rains heavily at night, and the morning is cold and gray.

We continue east. Toward evening, on a plain streaked with sunlight, about two thousand gazelles flee from several men on horseback. We camp nearby. Why are the gazelle here? I collect a sample of fresh droppings for microscopic food habit analysis, and also various plants, especially such grasses as *Poa, Stipa, Andropogon,* and *Cleistogenes,* to determine their protein and other nutrient contents.

We note that many females are heavily pregnant. We are just in time for the birth season.

On the way to Choibalsan, we stop at the county town of Sergelen. There we make a ritual visit to the main store to check out what is for sale: two bottles of beer and three of vodka, five dresses, three pairs of shoes, some matches and a little sugar, several bars of soap, and three loaves of bread. We buy one of the last-named. Nearby is a lake, Yakhoya Nuur. A telephone line extends south to Choibalsan and we follow it. Lacking trees in which to build nests, upland hawks have piled sticks, bones, and rags at the base of some telephone poles in which to lay eggs and raise young. The nests are clearly vulnerable to predators such as dogs and foxes, yet of the five nests we saw all contained young, some of them well-feathered.

As in UB, the foreign community in Choibalsan has expanded. The German Technical Assistance has even constructed its own building, where I meet Henry Mix, a colleague from Germany. At the UNDP office, Andrew Laurie introduces me to a tall young American with whom I will work on many field projects: Kirk Olson, who had recently arrived to study gazelles and obtain a graduate degree, although at present he has neither gotten a research grant nor been accepted into a university program. But his ability and persistence enabled him to join the Wildlife Conservation Society and the UNDP Steppe Project, and in 2008 he received his Ph.D. from the University of Massachusetts under the guidance of Todd Fuller with a thesis on

Mongolian gazelles. While in Choibalsan, I also look up my former colleague Nerendorjim Ganbaatar, from a local conservation society and hunting organization, who has been involved with gazelles since 1981. Our conversation roams over such topics as the commercial gazelle hunts and gazelle diseases, among them a *Pasteurella* bacterial infection that killed thousands in 1986.

We drive southwest toward an area where, we have been told, gazelles go to calve. The weather is miserable, and a harsh wind buffets the car. We stop at a ger and ask for directions. Four dogs huddle against the outside wall. Our host confirms that there are many gazelles not far away, near a Russian military base that was destroyed by the Mongolians in 1991. We're also told that the Russians killed many gazelles for food. Our host suggests that we spend the night in his storage ger, and we accept the invitation with pleasure. I fall asleep beneath several sheep carcasses suspended from the ceiling.

We wake up to another raw day and crowd around the dung fire in the ger all morning. Lhagva had observed newborn gazelles in this region in 1989; that year the first was sighted on June 15. We now drive out in search of herds. Seeing gazelles in the distance we continue on foot. As we top a rise, the steppe before us vibrates with gazelles in the soft light. There must be twenty-five thousand of them extending to the horizon. Not a building, not a fence, not a motor disrupts the harmony and stillness. I feel an exquisite pleasure and embrace a sense of oneness with the steppe. We do not want to disrupt the peaceful scene, and decide to return another day to look for newborns.

June 22. A shaky, wet head peers above the grass, alert, ears erect. It is 6:30 a.m., and the youngster was born within the past hour. Its mother had been lying with it but she ran from us, and now watches nearby. She has not yet expelled the afterbirth, judging by a strand of umbilical cord trailing from her vulva. We do not disturb the two further, but decide to come back soon to weigh and sex the young and clamp a small numbered tag into one of its ears to help us with recognition. When we return to the site three hours later, the calf has gone, but a female watches us alertly from about a thousand feet away. The young is near her, its coat now dry. As I draw closer, the baby gazelle crouches motionless, ears laid back. Kneeling before it, our faces almost touching, I look into its dark, unblinking eyes. Mine is only the second face it has seen in its short life. What are its thoughts? The calf bleats but does not struggle when Lhagva picks it up and places it into a cloth bag for weighing. Twigs of sage in the bag will, we hope, hide human body odor. The newborn is a male, weighing 9.5 pounds (4.3 kg). When replaced on the spot from which we picked him up, he crouches and we retreat.

In migratory or nomadic species such as the Mongolian gazelle, in which herds are constantly on the move, a young animal must be able to follow its mother soon after birth and stay close to her. If it becomes separated, it will starve because no other female is likely to permit an unknown young to suckle. I observed, for instance, a young running to an approaching female. They sniffed noses, and then she sniffed the youngster's rump. Abruptly she turned away, and it ran on through the herd searching for its mother.

To illustrate how fast a newborn develops, here are two examples from my field notes, observed from a distance with a scope:

1. A female licks her newborn at 0937. Its head is wet and part of the amniotic sac covers its back. At 0940, the young raises its head shakily. Seventeen minutes later, the female lowers her head to the young, which tries to stand up but topples over. The female licks the amniotic tissue off its back. Twice more during the next 40 minutes the young tries to rise but falls over backwards. Finally at the age of 75 minutes the young stands and shakily stumbles toward its mother 4 m

away. Immediately it searches for and finds the udder and suckles 25 seconds. She moves aside 3 m and it follows, walking with a hunched back, and suckles another 25 seconds. At 1052 the mother moves 100 m away, possibly nervous because of our car parked at a distance. The young follows her in a stumbling run, yet moving surprisingly well at the age of only about 90 minutes. Fifteen minutes later, when the young has settled down, we catch it, and weigh it—a female at 10.5 lbs [4.8 kg]. On being released, the young runs to its waiting mother.

2. A female flees from our car, the head of an infant protruding from her vulva. She trots about 600 m and lies down, only to move another 200 m away. A yearling female approaches and nuzzles her head. At 1325 [1:25 p.m.] she rises, turns, and lies again. At 1330 she turns her head several times and seems to lick something, but grass obscures our view. A male gazelle comes to within 10 m but veers aside when the female stands up facing him. She turns to lick her new-born for one minute. At the age of 22 minutes the newborn raises its head and two minutes later tries to stand but collapses onto its side. At 1427, at the age of 57 minutes, the young stands and walks several steps by its resting mother. Nine minutes later, when the female stands up, the young is quite steady as it circles her once. At 1452, the female begins to graze. The young approaches its mother from the side and suckles a few seconds, and 3 minutes later for 25 seconds while the mother nuzzles its rump. Both lie. At 1500, both leave the birth site. The young, 90 minutes old, gives several bounds as it follows. It is a male weighing 8.9 lbs [4 kg].

On subsequent days we find more young, their tan crouched forms making them easy to spot. But as we soon learned they can run fast and far within hours after birth. We needed a new technique to approach them. I now try walking slowly closer and stopping in full view. Meanwhile Lhagva approaches stealthily from the other side

*A newborn Mongolian gazelle crouches in the grass
waiting for its mother's return.*

and then crawls closer on hands and knees until he is in a position to
pounce. Sometimes he is successful; at other times the young bolts
just before being grabbed. On subsequent trips we brought a dip net,
as used by fishermen, to scoop up the young. For the first three days
or so of its life the young tends to be a "hider," lying motionless. After
that, for several days it will be a "waiter," lying down but alert, waiting until its mother returns but also ready to flee and even to wander
around a bit. Finally, after a week or so, it becomes a "follower," staying close to its mother.

The calving period of gazelles in a herd is highly synchronous,
as it is for caribou, chiru, and other migratory ungulates. After we
had observed the first young on June 22, about 90 percent were born
within twelve days. However, a few females still had not given birth
by July 10. The reasons for such synchrony are complex. Newborns

Lhagva stalks a crouched gazelle young to capture it for weighing and tagging.

are vulnerable to predation in the open terrain. By, in effect, flooding an area with young, the herd ensures that fewer are likely to be killed than if the births are spread over many months. Births, furthermore, occur in late spring, after the passing of the severe winter and at a time when nutritious young plants provide forage. This enables females to regain weight lost during winter, which helps the fetus grow, and then provide ample milk for the growing young.

We catch and examine young almost daily, and by season's end have information on a total of eighty-eight. The sex ratio is equal. The newborns average a little under 9 pounds (4 kg) in weight with males tending to be about half a pound heavier than the females.

With so much new life there is also death. One female, for example, runs from me, circles, and then watches from a distance. My search reveals a dead young lying on its side, still warm. I collect two ticks from its body and then autopsy it. There are deep puncture

Kirk Olson (left) *and Daria Odonkhuu weigh a newborn gazelle young.*

wounds in its groin and chest, with much internal bleeding, and the wound smells bad, indicating a massive infection. The conclusion: the young was attacked by a steppe eagle, golden eagle, or a cinereous vulture, managed to escape, but then died of infection.

A female occasionally dies in childbirth. We find a female lying dead on her side with the infant's head emerged from the birth canal. Now we have the sad task of performing an autopsy. The total weight of mother and calf is 67.1 pounds (30.5 kg). One foreleg of the infant is bent at a strange angle in the female's body, preventing the young from sliding out and the female from expelling it. The bone marrow of the female is quite fatty, indicating that she has not starved, though there is little fat around her internal organs. Marrow that is red and gelatinous signifies depletion of the body's fat reserves. The first molar tooth of her lower jaw has the heavy wear of an animal somewhat past its prime.

Mammalian predators are rather scarce on the calving grounds.

Hunters on the eastern steppe have butchered two Mongolian gazelles for food.

There are some dogs and foxes, and Andrew Laurie told me of finding the remains of four young gazelles at a wolf den. Human predators, however, are pervasive. We find a site where two female gazelles and a male have been butchered, all in their prime, judging by the discarded heads. These females probably each had a young waiting patiently for the return of its mother until it finally died. Another time we spot two men by their horses. We drive closer and then walk over to check. They have shot two male gazelles, the hides and chunks of meat spread on the ground. Lhagva scolds them. They reply that they need the meat for naadam, the upcoming national holiday. One man has a rifle and his wristband holds .22 caliber bullets. Lhagva reaches out to examine the rifle. The man backs off and draws a sheath knife. "Take my horse but not my rifle," he says. They then gather the gazelle parts, stuff them into plastic bags and tie them behind the saddle before riding away. Later the same day we spot a jeep driving slowly cross-country, obviously hunting. Through my scope I can see that the back of the jeep is full of dead gazelles. The jeep races off as we drive closer.

Male gazelles tend to separate from the females during the calving season and may congregate in herds of up to a hundred or more. However, some males remain with the females and cause disruption. I watch one male as he follows a female closely, his neck and head stretched upward. He displays his large goiter, which also functions as an echo chamber for his hollow grunts. Is he courting? Perhaps the scent of parturition resembles that of estrus. Her newborn lies nearby. She returns to it and the male follows. Rising shakily to its feet, the newborn totters beneath the male as if to suckle. The male jerks his horns at the infant and slashes with both forelegs, then follows the female again. She circles back to her young and nuzzles its rump as it tries to suckle. The persistent male advances again, rears bolt upright behind the female four times as if to mount and finally drifts away.

Such male harassment of females does not always end well. I found a dead female with a full-term fetus. Cause of death: a deep puncture wound just below the ribcage that resulted in massive internal bleeding. The 10-inch-deep hole was no doubt made by the horn of an aggressive and impatient male.

The birth season is almost over on July 10. Of the adult females tallied in mid-June, 96 percent were pregnant, and now only about 4 percent are waiting to give birth. It is time for us to leave. Working long days, we have weighed and sexed young, autopsied dead gazelles, collected fecal and plant specimens, and gathered other facts to help us gain the kind of insights necessary for the management and conservation of the gazelles. We still have much to learn, and as I leave Mongolia in July, my plan is to return for the calving season next year.

But as it turns out, the gazelles present a new issue, and I find myself back in Mongolia on November 2 for a three-week stay. Andrew Laurie had notified me in early September that gazelles were dying in large numbers. I was busy with projects in Tibet and Sarawak and could not come immediately. Once I arrive, we consider what disease might be affecting the animals. In the early 1960s many gazelles died from hoof-and-mouth disease, probably transmitted by livestock. Lhagva and I now fly to Choibalsan. There the veterinarian D. Nyamsuren of the Dornod Veterinary Clinic informs us that the gazelles have died of foot rot (*Fusobacterium necrophorum*), a bacterial infection caused by heavy summer rains. (The July rains were three times heavier than average.) The bacteria invade the sodden, softened feet, causing them to swell just above the hoof. This cuts off the blood supply and ultimately leads to gangrene. The gazelles hobble along on their infected, painful feet, trying to forage, until they lie down, never to rise.

Many gazelles died in the north, we are told, as well as to the east and southeast. With our driver Batsaihan, Lhagva and I head into the field. Soon we find gazelle bodies strewn over the steppe, in some places a lone animal, and at others a cluster of animals, as if gathered for a communal death. Most bodies have been reduced to a skeleton encased in a hide, the rest consumed by maggots. Few have been touched by scavengers such as foxes, ravens, or upland hawks. Examining the gazelles, I take note of the lesions and the swellings above the hooves, often just on one or both of the front legs. We record the sex and collect the lower jaw, or at least an incisor, to enable us to determine age at death. The bone marrow tells us something about the animal's nutritional condition. Most evenings we return to Choibalsan reeking of the distinctive odor of rotten and maggot-eaten carcasses.

The veterinarian William (Billy) Karesh from the Wildlife Conservation Society arrives within a few days. This outbreak of foot rot has been a reminder that disease may have a sudden and capricious impact on a wildlife population. Billy has come to evaluate all evidence of infectious disease in the gazelles by checking blood and tissues, and, importantly, to compare the results with those found in domestic animals. We now collaborate with Andrew Laurie and others from the UNDP office, with veterinarian Nyamsuren, and with the director of protected areas Dr. N. Tseveenmyadag to look into issues concerning these gazelle diseases.

By November 16, we have examined 447 dead gazelles, a large enough sample for some tentative conclusions. Sectioning the incisor teeth to count age rings shows us that females had on average a longer life than the males. About 28 percent of females died of foot rot between the ages of 6 and 10, whereas only one male out of thirty-six reached the age of 6. Zhaowen Jiang and his team in their study found that the oldest gazelle at death they examined in Inner Mongolia was 7.5 years old. The bone marrow of females was, as expected, depleted of fat after the stresses of pregnancy, lactation, and foot rot, and young animals also had been starving. By contrast, most adult males still had some fat.

Our counts in previous years showed that about half the young born in June and July survive into winter. But now our counts indicate that only 11 percent of the adult females had a young at heel. The disease deaths do not include an unusually large number of young. Where are they? Did they die elsewhere on the steppe? Yearlings born in 1997 had died in disproportionately large numbers, at least three times more than expected. So, as in any project, we blunder around hoping that the facts we collect will help us understand the species.

June–July 1999

I arrived back in UB on June 18, 1999, eager to monitor another gazelle calving season, and within three days flew to Choibalsan. There Lhagva and Kirk meet me, as does Vadim Kiriliuk, a Russian gazelle researcher who will join us on occasion. The gazelles are in the same area as last year, I'm informed, but instead of being in large herds they are now in small scattered ones. This is perhaps because this year is dry and succulent forage is scarce. The birth season begins on June 23. In a timely arrival the following day, Billy Karesh and his colleague Sharon Deem join us to collect blood from the newborns. For a few days after birth a young gazelle retains the disease antibodies of its mother. Without having to capture adult gazelles, we can learn what infectious diseases the population has been exposed to. Billy and Sharon also collected samples from domestic sheep and goats.

In brief, it was found that gazelles and domestic stock share antibodies to various diseases that under certain conditions can lead to major outbreaks. Both share the parainfluenza-3 and bovine respiratory viruses, which are known to cause respiratory disease in livestock. Gazelles also have antibodies to a herpes virus, infectious bovine rhinotracheitis. We also found the bovine diarrhea virus in both gazelles and livestock. Stillbirths and deaths among newborns have been associated with this virus in white-tailed deer in North America. The highly contagious virus for foot-and-mouth disease was only noted in domestic sheep. Both the livestock and gazelles tested positive for the poxvirus, which is transmitted by direct contact and may cause serious and even fatal skin eruptions. Autopsies of adult gazelles showed various pathologic lesions and tumors, and, Sharon Deem and her colleagues wrote, "We know of no other free-ranging populations of ungulates with such a high incidence." This important disease survey emphasizes the need to monitor the health of both the gazelle and livestock populations.

Our daily task of observing the newborns and their mothers continues. By July 12 all but a few females have given birth. More and more females now take their hidden young to join herds. On July 6 some 65 percent of adult females have a calf at heel; by July 12 the figure is 84 percent. For unexplained reasons, few calves survived last year, but this year most females have an offspring. Several heavy showers have turned the steppe green and lush, offering nutritious forage at a critical time. The blood samples Billy and Sharon collected from the young revealed an interesting change during the day. Those taken during the morning hours showed a high fat level, which had disappeared by noon. Fat levels go up after eating, and a newborn typically suckles in the morning and then again when the mother returns after having been away feeding. A female on a starvation diet has little or no milk with adequate fat content to pass on to her offspring.

Each year seems to bring a new problem for the gazelles. Kirk and I are out monitoring the gazelle herds when powerful lightning bolts strike the steppe. Soon we note the red glow of a grass fire beyond a ridge in the direction of our camp. The fire creeps closer, and we must move our tents to another site. But again the fire pursues us, slithering through the dry grass almost unnoticed, then flaring up when it consumes a tall grass tuft.

Soon our camp is a grass island surrounded by scorched steppe and a wall of smoke. Newborn gazelles lie hidden in the feather grass throughout the area. Concerned about them, I go for a long, lone walk following the edge of grass and burn. Ahead a young gazelle crouches as wind-driven fire crackles closer and closer. When the flames almost touch the young, it flees about 130 feet (40 m) into the grass and crouches down again. Another young stumbles from the fire's edge, its rump scorched black. Yet it crouches again near the fire, retreats again, and lies down until flames almost touch it. At my approach a calf darts right through the flames onto the burn, wheels around, and hides once more in the grass. These and other young showed no fear of the smoke and flames, although they finally escaped when the in-

A steppe fire almost scorches a crouched gazelle young before it flees.

tense heat singed their hair. Each seemed hesitant to move from the place where it had been left by its mother. Several females are nearby, but not one goes to a calf to lead it to safety.

On subsequent days we check the burned area for young killed by the fire. There is only one, its rump blackened, though it may have been killed and partially eaten by one of the steppe eagles loitering in the area. Not until we drive around do we realize the extent of the burn, a block of steppe of about 3,080 square miles (8,000 km²). Females and young now gather into large nursery herds of hundreds and even thousands. Youngsters come together, resting and playing in groups of up to twenty. Mothers search for their offspring, wandering through the herd, and occasionally stop and yip. And young look for their mothers, dashing up to females and after a mutual sniff moving on.

The birth season is over, and it is time for us to make plans to return next year, this time with radio-collars that will enable us to track the gazelles during their nomadic wanderings.

June–July 2000

I came back to Choibalsan on June 23, 2000, this time with Kay, and we met with Lhagva, Kirk, Andrew, Daria, and other old friends and field colleagues. The next day, after a five-hour drive, we arrive at our field camp, sited in the same area as last year. Two gers have been set up, one for cooking and one for sleeping, and Kay and I erect our own tent. The steppe has a flush of green after several rains, and short-toed larks are in full song. Gazelles dot the steppe in small herds. The first birth was recorded on June 21, and 90 percent of the adult females are still pregnant, heralding a flood of young soon. Within two days we have radio-collars on ten newborns, four males, and six females. The collars are expandable so they will not restrict the neck as the young gazelle grows. The transmitters are VHF, which in this open terrain should transmit a signal to our receiver and directional handheld antenna for some 6 to 12 miles (10–20 km) or more. The transmitter also has a motion sensor, which indicates by the speed of the beeps whether the calf is quietly at rest or active.

Now our real work begins. We have to find each young gazelle we tagged every day and determine its precise location without disturbing it. We also need to monitor activity of the young day and night. This we do, with everyone helping for eight continuous days from June 26 to July 3. Fortunately we could receive transmitter signals from several young at the same time, until each dispersed with its mother. Thus we collected 3,799 readings, one for each animal every fifteen minutes. Daria, Kirk, and their colleagues, who summarized these data in 2009 ("Activity, Movements, and Sociality of Newborn Mongolian Gazelle Calves in the Eastern Steppe"), showed that gazelle young tend to be most active at sunrise and sunset, when they are probably suckled by their mother. They are least active in late morning, when they crouch while their mother is away feeding.

Overall, as a young gazelle increases in age it becomes more active, from 18 percent of the twenty-four-hour day at the age of two days, and 29 percent at seven days, to 54 percent at twenty-five days, when it travels with its mother. We have been aware of the speed at which a young can run within a few days of birth. But as revealed by the radio signals, they also travel much more than I would have guessed. To quote Daria Odonkhuu and his coauthors from their paper: "By days 5–8, calves had moved an average of 6.6 km (range 2–21 km) from capture sites … but were still only seen alone or with their mother. By days 24–26, however, they were located an average of 41 km (range 24–63 km) away from their capture sites." A move of up to 39 miles, or 63 kilometers, from the birth site is most impressive! The youngster must also learn to socialize and stay close to its mother after the first week of life, when it may suddenly be surrounded by a throng of hundreds of gazelles. The team collared eight more young in 2001 and kept track of them for close to 185 days until the following January. Each calf was by then 83–128 miles (134–206 km) from its birth site. Even though they were born in the same area, the young did not stay together. "The greatest distance between simultaneous locations of two marked calves was 161 miles (260 km)," as a research paper by Kirk Olson, Todd Fuller, and others, "Annual Movements of Mongolian Gazelles," notes.

To obtain even more detail about the movements of gazelle, the team captured four adult females in September 2003, an effort in which I did not participate. These females were fitted with Argos satellite-collars programmed to transmit one location per day for about a year. The range sizes of these females varied greatly during different seasons; they traveled the least distance during the calving and winter seasons. Females that were captured together subsequently showed little range overlap. Here is the travel information of the female with transmitter number 41599, as presented in the research paper by Kirk Olson, Todd Fuller, and others. At calving season her range was 140 square miles (363 km²), in spring 2,299 square miles (5,954 km²), during the summer 1,182 square miles (3,061 km²), in autumn 6,639 square miles (17,195 km²), and in winter 925 square miles (2,396 km²). The female's total range was 11,873 square miles (30,751 km²), but as the authors point out that figure represents only about 6.5 percent of the whole steppe area. Such seasonal shifts suggest that there is a change in either habitat quality or nutritional requirements of the gazelle or both. Since the gazelle do not reveal any regular migratory pattern, being instead nomadic, roaming from place to place with little obvious pattern, it is likely that the availability of forage also changes from year to year. In this the gazelle differ from, for example, the Tibetan antelope, a species whose females, but not males, have specific migratory routes to and from their calving ground. But like the Mongolian gazelle they have a short, discrete birth season in late June, and newborns develop rapidly and follow their mother.

Our analysis of plant remains in gazelle dung reveals that the animals eat a wide variety of species, particularly various grasses, wild onions, the forb *Potentilla,* and the branch tips of the low shrubs *Caragana* and the sage *Artemisia.* These species are also favored by livestock, pointing to direct competition between them. To understand the pattern of gazelle movement, one needs to understand about vegetation productivity. What attracts gazelles to certain areas? Kirk once saw an aggregation of about two hundred thousand gazelles. Thomas Mueller, Kirk, and their colleagues used satellite imagery to answer this question, as related in their 2008 scientific paper "In Search of

Forage." The satellite measures primary plant productivity using what is called the Normalized Difference Vegetation Index (NDVI). The results show a complex pattern of biomass on the steppe. As they wrote, "Gazelles preferred an intermediate range of vegetation productivity, presumably facing quality-quantity trade-offs where areas with low NDVI are limited by ingestion rates, and areas with high NDVI are limited by low digestibility of mature forage." They concluded that preferred gazelle habitats thus varied greatly by place and season, even if one does not take into consideration other factors such as high livestock densities and commercial development. "Only about 15% of the study area was consistently gazelle habitat throughout the study period, indicating that gazelles need to range over vast areas in search of food," they wrote. Furthermore, research by E. V. Rotshild, among others, has shown that the level of trace metals, such as of copper, zinc, and vanadium, in forage may stimulate or depress the growth of disease organisms in an animal, another reason for gazelles to roam widely.

In sum, from these statistics and data we can see that only detailed and creative regional planning for the whole steppe landscape can save this magnificent gazelle population in its sublime remoteness. Planning must take into account the threats of development, shifting forage availability, barriers to movement, and competition with livestock. Planners will also need to monitor the health, fertility, and mortality of the gazelles and their habitat.

8

A Return to Great Father Sky

It is understandable that the actions directed toward improving the quality of human life and conserving the earth's vitality and diversity require significant financial resources. However, since we are speaking about our only home, the earth, and about the fate of human civilization, the only reasonable thing to do is to mobilize all available and potential resources.

After all, the problem is not the money, but our resolve and readiness to make decisions that will bring humanity out of this dead end situation, and into a world of sustainable resources. Only by doing this, will we be worthy of civilization and stewardship of the earth's environment, which we have inherited.

Mongolia's Minister for Nature and
Environment Zamba Batjargal, 2007

I longed to return to the great eastern steppes, to see the luminous morning sun spilling over the grassland that stretches toward a limitless horizon, to watch herds of tawny Mongolian gazelles streaming past, to be part again of the Great Father Sky and the luxurious feeling of freedom and solitude. I had heard that oil and mining development had increased greatly on the steppe during the previous decade. "There is nothing permanent except change," said the Greek philosopher Heraclitus some 2,500 years ago. And today one must also ask if "there is nothing immune from the pressures and destruction of development." As my flight lands in UB on June 18, 2018, I wonder about changes that have occurred over the past decade, when I was away from Mongolia. Kirk Olson meets me and takes me to his home on a hillside overlooking UB, a grassy slope on which some marmots persist. There I am warmly greeted by his wife, Oyuna, and daughter, Ocean, who is just starting school. I'm astonished at the size of UB, stretching for miles along the Tuula River valley. There are many blocks of new apartment buildings and some structures are twenty stories or more tall. The population of UB is now 1.5 million, half the country's total number.

When I go into UB the following day, I realize that it has become a major metropolis. Traffic congestion is overwhelming, and parking spaces are difficult to find. Many cars are shiny, new, and expensive. Shops selling exclusive European brands crowd the thoroughfares, and grocery stores overflow with goods onto the sidewalks. Now few Mongolians wear traditional clothes, the ankle-length deel for women and the wraparound, long-sleeved gown tied with a broad sash for men. UB has achieved its resurrection after the calamitous early 1990s. This was truly evident when I wandered through a seven-story department store, each floor crowded with clothes, food, toys, electronics, and much else. In the town's central square, the hero Damdin Sukhbaatar, who fought for Mongolia's independence, still sits astride his prancing horse, but the massive mausoleum of dictator Choibalsan has been moved elsewhere.

Kirk takes me to the Wildlife Conservation Society's Mongolia office, where he also occupies a desk. Enkhtuvshin Shiilegdamba, a veterinarian known as Enkee, capably manages a staff of about twenty, its work focused on wildlife, habitat, and community studies. Jambal Sergelenkhuu, Seegii for short, a botanist, presents me with her book

Flowers of Hustai National Park. It is an invaluable field guide to an area into which the Przewalski's horse has been reintroduced. And I am delighted to meet Dashka, Jachliin Tserendeleg's son, again. He works for WCS, and his brother Purev is the director of Hustai Nuruu National Park. Both sons are carrying on the great conservation tradition of their father, something that would have made him immensely proud. Aili Kang, my colleague on half a dozen trips in China, drops by. She is now in charge of managing Central Asian projects at the WCS office in New York. She will join Kirk and me for a look at the eastern steppes, and afterward we will proceed to Tibet with Cristian Samper, the president and CEO of WCS. Also coming with us to the steppes is Bolortsetseg Sanjaa from this WCS office. Marvelously efficient, she becomes a valuable addition to our team, helping with all tasks from cooking to wildlife observation.

We head east on June 21, Kirk driving his old Jeep station wagon. Our aim is to traverse the steppe to its eastern tip at the Nomrog Strictly Protected Area, and then loop back to UB by another route. We pass a huge coal mine near the city, and soon are in rolling rangelands, the grass stubble a desiccated tan because of drought and heavy grazing by untended livestock. We camp by the Kherlen River at dusk. The following morning we continue toward the provincial capitals of Undur Khaan and Baruun-Urt. Round spiderwebs stretched flat on the ground and covered with dew glisten in the sun. We stop to scan the sunlit steppe from a rise, and in all directions it rolls on, with the only human signs two gers.

We stop in the county town of Matad to buy gasoline and some supplies. When I was here in 1993, the town was without electricity, gasoline was unavailable, and the "supermarket" shelves were empty. I now check labels on packages in a grocery store, its shelves fully stocked. Some items are of Mongolian manufacture, but most have been imported from China and Russia, and some from Germany. There are also biscuits from Indonesia, orange juice from Iran, and chocolate bars from Argentina. Mongolia has certainly become part of the global market economy, an impressive change in just two decades.

Our visit to this particular area has another purpose. Kirk has been informed that many gazelles died here in June and July 2017 of an unknown disease or, perhaps, because of the drought. It was unlikely to have been the foot rot that killed so many gazelles in 1998. We have the approximate location of the die-off, and a family in a ger directs us to a stony hill on the steppe. We camp there, our GPS giving coordinates of 47° 13′ N, 115° 28.5′ E. We find gazelle bodies immediately the next morning. Females lie scattered on the rocky hillside, their bodies now just bones encased in dry hide. Foxes and vultures have ripped some carcasses open, but most rest as they have died. Some are alone, but others lie together as if seeking comfort in death; some are in a crouch and others have legs rigidly extended. The hollow bodies are the retreats of gray moths, which flutter out in swarms when disturbed by us as we check the teeth for eruption and wear to determine a gazelle's approximate age. The deaths happened exactly a year ago during the birth season. As we roam over the melancholy hill, we are increasingly saddened at finding so many dead newborns. Some of these had crowded together. One rock cleft has one female and eight calves piled on top of each other. At another site four newborns died with their legs intertwined, as if seeking solace. By early afternoon we have examined 252 bodies on this one hill, and we have been told that there are other such sites. There is only one male among the dead, his horns and teeth indicating an age of two years.

What disease caused this mass death during the birth season? Kirk collects bone marrow from some skeletons in the hope of identifying the agent in a laboratory. But he suspects it to be a viral disease called PPR (peste des petits ruminants), which spread out of Africa and is known to have also killed saiga antelope in Mongolia. The symptoms are fever, diarrhea, and mouth sores. The 2018 gazelle birth season has already begun. The day after examining the carcasses, we see two small herds of female gazelles and among them four newborns. With so many infected gazelle remains scattered over the steppe, we can only wish the new generation good luck.

Continuing east we soon come upon an oil development stretching far along a broad and shallow valley at 47° 57′ N and 116° 12′ E. Row upon row of derricks slowly lower and raise their bulbous heads. It is one of a number of developments by Petro-China, consisting of clusters of barracks, sheds, and storage tanks. The laborers are Chinese. Convoys of Chinese tanker trucks deliver the oil south to China for refining.

On June 25, we come upon a huge agricultural development. The coordinates of the site are 47° 31′ N and 118° 34′ E, if anyone wants to check up on it at some future date. The development is spread over 1,158 square miles (3,000 km²). Mongolia grows only about 30 percent of the wheat it needs and must import the rest. By plowing up the steppe, the government hopes to increase production. Some fields here have sprouts whereas others lie fallow. Large tillers slice up more rangeland. Tractors spread pesticides. I'm aghast! Has Mongolia learned nothing from its neighbor in Inner Mongolia, or has the government conveniently preferred to ignore all the evidence? The steppe is a gentle landscape without natural defenses against plow and plunder. Mongolia is blundering toward disaster. After plowing up its rangelands, neighboring Inner Mongolia has suffered from widespread desertification, erosion, and severe yellow dust storms, which engulf Beijing and the region as a whole. As a 1992 report of the National Research Council noted about Inner Mongolia's rangelands: "Compared to 1965,... deteriorated grasslands have increased by 28.7 million hectares, and total grass production has dropped by 30%." What are today's statistics? I pick up a handful of plowed soil. It's nothing but dry powder in my hand, and a strong gust of wind blows it away. Ahead, toward one end of a field, are several dust twisters funneling skyward, another premonition of the future. Adding to the danger, climate change is seriously affecting Mongolia. Summer and winter temperatures are more extreme, and severe droughts affect water supplies. The UNDP has implemented a major project to help communities use its scarce water more sustainably. Yet before me the desertification of the country continues unchecked.

Once the steppe has been plowed up, the subtle interdependence of its many plant and animal species will be permanently disrupted. Some species have already died, particularly various soil organisms; some have moved away; and new ones have invaded. The steppe will never recover its original state. Will the country at least spare a fragment of this precious steppe from development, and favor preservation over profit?

After a stretch of wide-open steppe, the grass tall and free of livestock, we approach the county town of Sumber (Halhgol), located near the Nomrog Strictly Protected Area. Here we meet L. Myagmasuren, who was our guide in 2002. Kirk, who speaks fluent Mongolian, queries him about current wildlife conditions in Nomrog. Fishing for taimen and other species is still unregulated, he notes, and the Nomrog River is polluted by pesticides from China, but, on a positive note, moose and other deer populations have increased owing to their better protection.

During our 2002 visit we had been told of two iron mines that were already located within the buffer zone of Nomrog. A new mine was started in 2008. And there is a wheat field in the buffer zone as well. We stop near a border post to look at the new bridge that was built across the Nomrog River. Once the planned railroad and Millennial Highway reach here, iron ore, coal, and other resources can easily be exported to China. A burly Mongolian soldier accompanies us to the bridge, an attractive structure with an imposing entry arch and golden sculptures of small neighing, rearing, and galloping horses on the railings. The international border is halfway across the bridge. Several young Chinese wave to us from their side, and we wave back.

I am naturally concerned about the continual creeping intrusion of mining companies into protected areas. As John Farrington, a conservationist, noted in a 2005 article: "At present, mining is the Mongolia government's single most important source of tax revenue. . . . However, if Mongolia's protected areas are to function as intended and achieve their objective of preserving the nation's environmental resources for the benefit of future generations of Mongolians, relevant laws concerning protected areas and mining must be enforced."

After checking in with the border police and obtaining a travel permit, we head back west toward UB. As usual we camp on the steppe. We all set up our own tents and help with the communal one. Kirk and Sanjaa like to cook. With a glass of wine in hand before dinner, we share experiences and dreams beneath Great Father Sky in an area devoid of humans except us. I rise shortly after 4:00 with the first light. It's windy and chilly, and I huddle in the car to write up notes. After breakfast, we are back on the road by 7:00.

On crossing a rise, we see bales of hay, hundreds of them, scattered over the steppe. We are at 47° 36′ N and 117° 09′ E. The hay, we learn, was cut in late August nearly a year ago and never picked up. Haying took place over an area of 115 square miles (300 km²). About 400,000 tons per year are cut for export to China. The bales are massive, about 6 × 4 × 4.5 feet. Exposed to all kinds of weather for nearly a year, they are also disintegrating. Repeated haying has no doubt an adverse impact on the rangelands. A range will deteriorate if more than 60 percent of its annual production is removed. Taking away the grass cover dries the soil and exposes it to wind erosion. This depletes the organic nutrients in the soil. Consequently the roots of grasses may wither, depriving them of access to moisture below the surface of the baked ground. The hungry mouths of livestock may also pull the weakened plants up by the roots. With the death of grasses, the rangelands will become a barren plain covered in places only with determined weeds.

We continue westward to Choibalsan, still named after the murderous dictator. The buildings that had been destroyed in the early 1990s have been cleared away, and many new apartment blocks have sprung up. The Nomin Megastore, located in a converted carpet factory, has a vast assortment of items for sale, including five wolf skins. Not far west of town we come upon herd after herd of Mongolian gazelles. Most of the herds are small, but there is one with about two thousand gazelles and another of five thousand. The gazelles are shy, shyer than I remembered them from previous years, moving away on perceiving our car. Most are females, and some have newborns at heel. By revealing about nine thousand of its gazelles, the steppe could not have given me a more glorious farewell gift.

As we continue toward UB, I ponder our observations concerning resource development on the steppe. Our trip has lasted only ten days, but we were able to see the impact of mining, oil drilling, haying, and tilling. I know, of course, that big business with its special interest dollars rules every country, including the politicians who make the decisions about what to exploit. Can governments become enlightened and integrate ecological values into their decisions to create a humane and equitable world, one that is economically and environmentally sustainable? Mongolia has over sixty parliamentary laws and government policy documents concerning nature conservation. The casual way in which these are circumvented, however, suggests that the people feel no collective responsibility. I have given many examples in this book. Genghis Khan seemed to have had a greater ecological conscience, a deeper feeling for the environment, judging by his rulings, than do most of today's politicians. My comments are not designed to demean a country that has treated me with such hospitality. I'm merely trying to rally its people to nature's defense, to inspire them to protect and manage the steppe and other ecosystems based on their knowledge and compassion. After all, the country's 1991 Constitution promises every citizen the right "to live in a safe and healthy environment." Mongolia has also committed itself to protecting 30 percent of the nation's land by 2030. I shall await the good news that it has achieved these grand goals.

Actually, Mongolia already has a fine system of protected areas. Will it persist? At present there are far too few guards to manage and protect them all. The guards are also underpaid and lack transport and other necessary equipment to do their job, something the government must correct to achieve its goals. Promotion of tourism would generate income, of which a considerable proportion could then be given to local communities to nurture a strong commitment to wildlife and habitat conservation.

But as we cross the steppe, its grasslands in part withered, overgrazed, or "developed," I naturally worry about the future. Bad weather, livestock diseases, and other problems have greatly affected the livelihood of herder households. Livestock depends on healthy pastures to provide a family with subsistence, offering meat, wool, milk, hides, dung, and transport, and it is often the sole source of cash income. I have discussed rangeland deterioration in various chapters of this book, especially Chapter 4. With so much of Mongolia's economy dependent on grasslands, its future, as my depressing observations on this trip attest, is in doubt. A 2006 publication by Douglas Johnson and his colleagues is worth quoting on various issues that remain highly relevant today:

> Mongolian rangelands are in a critical state of transition today. Nomadic pastoralism as a viable and productive form of land use in Mongolia is being questioned. During the last decade, a combination of increased livestock numbers, diminished spatial distribution of livestock because of broken wells, collapse of many grazing management systems, severe winter storms, and a series of drought years have significantly affected rangeland ecological condition and long-term ecological stability of rangeland resources across much of the country.... This situation has implications for the long-term sustainability of livelihoods among many herder households.

Changes in Mongolia in the past century have been drastic, it should be remembered. The country evolved from a Communist system with a centrally planned economy in which herders were ultimately forced to join a collective and all livestock was state owned to a market-based economy. The collectives were so unpopular that many herder families moved into towns. Then in 1992 the collectives were abolished and livestock became private property again. The numbers of both herder households and livestock increased dramatically. At the same time, households suddenly found themselves on their own, without grazing regulations, except for ineffective directives of local governments. Consequently, families tended to concentrate near water and population centers. "However, herders in Mongolia increasingly perceive that localized overstocking and especially lack of mobility are causing significant declines in the ecological condition and forage production," write Johnson and his colleagues. Severe overgrazing near communities remains conspicuous. As they note, "More people are engaged in livestock production and are dependent on livestock as a source of livelihood compared to the Socialist era."

The publication further states that "pastoral communities in Mongolia are currently unable to adequately respond to new paradigms that arise from government policies, environmental activism, changing production economics, and shifting food desires of an increasingly urbanized population. These changes are affecting the social, economic, and ecological sustainability of pastoral communities." The industrialization of the steppe will, as I noted, have a lasting impact on the habitat and the persistence of a livestock herding culture. And with climate change and its harsher weather the steppe will come under ever-increasing pressure. Grasslands such as these sequester an enormous amount of carbon. Their destruction, through their conversion to fields, for example, hastens climate change. Will Mongolia adapt its policies and management programs to retain a viable livestock production system? Will the great herds of Mongolian gazelles persist and continue to entrance tourists and locals? One concern is that there seems to be too little awareness by government departments and development agencies about the actual impact of their environmental decisions.

Back in UB, I check into the Khuvsgol Lake Hotel, now one of at least two dozen luxurious hotels. My room is on the twenty-third floor. It has a refrigerator with drinks, an electric coffeepot, a bathroom with hot water, and other amenities that make me feel rather dissolute when remembering the Spartan hotel conditions of a quarter-century earlier. I have to wait several days in town before heading to Tibet on July 4, a good opportunity to meet old friends and colleagues. Mongolia has become a magnet for foreign conservationists. Currently present is George Archibald of the International Crane Foundation. Dan Miller and I were companions on the uplands of Tibet's Chang Tang. Andrew Laurie, Richard Reading, Raul Valdez, and others all resurrect precious memories. Such get-togethers also give me an excuse to sample UB's many new restaurants—Sichuan, Indian, Korean, Japanese. Enkee and I visit the National Modern Art Gallery, and Seegii and I attend a concert of traditional Mongolian music, featuring throat singers with deep, rumbling voices and dancers wearing fierce masks. I note all this to show how greatly the town has changed in just a few years.

A special honor also awaits me. At a public meeting, arranged by the WCS, Minister Zamba Batjargal presents me with a medal, a government award: "Environmental outstanding employee of the Ministry of Nature and Tourism of Mongolia." The medal resembles the Mongolian flag: it is blue to represent the eternal sky and red to show freedom and progress. It also has on it the national emblem that symbolically incorporates fire, sun, moon, earth, and water. In addition, the society gives me a small silver bowl filled with fragments of dried cheese, a gesture of respect and welcome I have encountered when visiting a nomad family on the steppe. I treasure these last few days in UB, and, as always, anticipate a return to the Land of Grass and Gazelle, of Sun and Sky.

Appendix: Scientific Names of Species Referenced

The following are the scientific names of Mongolian mammals and birds mentioned in the text.

Mammals

Ground squirrel	*Spermophilus sp.*
Siberian marmot	*Marmota sibirica*
Hamster	*Cricetelus sp.*
Vole	*Microtus sp.*
Gerbil or jerboa	*Allactago sp.*
Zokor	*Myospalax sp.*
Hedgehog	*Hemiechinus dauricus*
Pika	*Ochotona sp.*
Tolai hare	*Lepus tolai*
Raccoon dog	*Nyctereutes procyonoides*
Steppe polecat	*Mustela eversmanni*
Pallas's cat	*Otocolobus manul*
Lynx	*Lynx lynx*
Snow leopard	*Panthera uncia*
Corsac fox	*Vulpes corsac*
Red fox	*Vulpes vulpes*
Wolf	*Canis lupus*
Brown bear	*Ursus arctos*
Przewalski's horse	*Equus Przewalskii*

Khulan (onager; Mongolian wild ass)	*Equus hemionus*
Wild Bactrian camel	*Camelus bactrianus ferus*
Wild pig	*Sus scrofa*
Roe deer	*Capreolus pygargus*
Red deer	*Cervus elaphus*
Moose	*Alces alces*
Black-tailed (goitered) gazelle	*Gazella subgutturosa*
Mongolian gazelle	*Procapra gutturosa*
Saiga antelope	*Saiga tatarica*
Ibex	*Capra sibirica*
Argali sheep	*Ovis ammon*

Birds

Chukar partridge	*Alectoris chuka*
Daurian partridge	*Perdix dauricae*
Black grouse	*Tetrao tetrix*
Demoiselle crane	*Grus virgo*
White-naped crane	*Grus vipio*
Great bustard	*Otis tarda*
Houbara bustard	*Chlamydotus undulate*
Pallas's sandgrouse	*Syrrhaptes paradoxus*
Northern lapwing	*Vanellus vanellus*
Black kite	*Milvu migrans*
Bearded vulture	*Gypaetus barbatus*
Cinereous vulture	*Aegypius monachus*
Common hawk	*Buteo buteo*
Upland hawk	*Buteo hemilasius*
Golden eagle	*Aquila chrysaetos*
Steppe eagle	*Aquila nipalensis*
Kestrel	*Falco tinnunculus*
Saker falcon	*Falco cherrug*

Cormorant	*Phalacrocorax sp.*
Carrion crow	*Corvus corone*
Raven	*Corvus corax*
Mongolian lark	*Melanocorypha mongolica*
Crested lark	*Galerida cristata*
Short-toed lark	*Calandrella brachydactyla*
Desert wheatear	*Oenanthe deserti*

Selected References

These references offer sources for material in the text, as well as further reading on the land and wildlife of Mongolia.

Andrews, Roy Chapman. *Ends of the Earth*. New York: Putnam's, 1929.

Andrews, Roy Chapman. *The New Conquest of Central Asia*. New York: American Museum of Natural History, 1932.

Arnold, Chris Feliciano. *The Third Bank of the River*. New York: Picador, 2018.

Barfield, Thomas. *The Perilous Frontier: Nomadic Empires of China*. Oxford: Basil Blackwell, 1989.

Batjargal, Zamba. *Fragile Environment, Vulnerable People and Sensitive Society*. Tokyo: Kaihatu-Shah, 2007.

Batsaikhan, Nyamsuren, Bayarbaatar Buuveibaatar, Bazaar Chimed, et al. "Conserving the World's Finest Grassland Amidst Ambitious National Development." *Conservation Biology* 28, no. 6 (2014): 1736–39.

Bawden, C. R. *The Modern History of Mongolia*. London: Kegan Paul, 1989.

Becker, Jasper. *The Lost Country: Mongolia Revealed*. London: Hodder and Stoughton, 1992.

Berger, Joel. *Extreme Conservation*. Chicago: University of Chicago Press, 2018.

Bruun, Ole, and Ole Odgaard, eds. *Mongolia in Transition: Old Patterns, New Challenges*. Richmond, UK: Curzon, 1996.

Chadwick, Douglas. *Tracking Gobi Grizzlies: Surviving Beyond the Back of Beyond*. Ventura, Calif.: Patagonia, 2017.

Clark, Emma L., and Munkhbat Javzansuren, comps. *Mongolian Red List of Mammals*. London: Zoological Society of London, 2006.

Deem, Sharon, William Karesh, and Michael Linn, et al. "Health Evaluation of Mongolian Gazelles, *Procapra gutturosa,* on the Eastern Steppes." *Gnusletter* (IUCN) 20, no. 1 (2001): 18–20, and 21, no. 1 (2002): 23–24.

Douglas, William O. "Journey to Outer Mongolia." *National Geographic Society* 121, no. 3 (1962): 289–343.

Farrington, J. D. "The Impact of Mining Activities on Mongolia's Protected Areas: A Status Report with Policy Recommendations." *Integrated Environmental Assessment and Management* 1, no. 3 (2005): 283–89.

Forrest, Jessica, Nikolai Sindorf, and Ryan Bartlett. *Guardians of the Headwaters.* Vol. 2: *Biodiversity, Water and Climate in Six Snow Leopard Landscapes.* Washington, D.C.: World Wildlife Fund Technical Report, 2017.

Galbreath, Gary, Colin Groves, and Lisette Waits. "Genetic Resolution of Composition and Phylogenetic Placement of the Isabelline Bear." *Ursus* 18, no. 1 (2007): 129–31.

Germeraad, Pieter W., and Zandangin Enebisch. *The Mongolian Landscape Tradition: A Key to Progress.* Schiedam, The Netherlands: BGS Schiedam, 1996.

Gwin, Peter. "Raiders of the Sky." *National Geographic* 234, no. 4 (2018): 98–121.

Hambly, Gavin, ed. *Central Asia.* New York: Delacorte, 1966.

Hare, John. "Ghost of the Gobi." *Wildlife Conservation* (New York) 101, no. 6 (1998): 24–29.

Hare, John, *The Lost Camels of Tartary.* London: Little, Brown, 1998.

Hedin, Sven. *Central Asia and Tibet.* 2 vols. London: Hurst and Blackett, 1903.

Jamsran, Undarmaa, Kenji Tamura, Natsagdorj Luvsan, and Norikazu Yamanaka, eds. *Rangeland Ecosystems of Mongolia.* Ulaan Baatar: Munkhiin Useg, 2018.

Jiang, Zhaowen, Seiki Takatsuki, Gao Zhongxin, and Jin Kun. "The Present Status, Ecology and Conservation of the Mongolian Gazelle, *Procapra gutturosa:* A Review." *Mammal Society* (Japan) 23, no. 1 (1998): 63–78.

Johansson, Orjan. "Unveiling the Ghost of the Mountain: Snow Leopard Ecology and Behaviour." Ph.D. diss., Swedish University of Agricultural Sciences, Uppsala, 2017.

Johnson, Douglas, Dennis Sheehy, Daniel Miller, and Daalkhaijav Damiran. "Mongolian Rangeland in Transition." *Secheresse* 17, nos. 1–2 (2006): 133–41.

Lattimore, Owen. *Nomads and Commissars.* New York: Oxford University Press, 1962.

Lhagvasuren, Badanjavin, and E. Milner-Gulland. "The Status and Management of the Mongolian Gazelle (*Procapra gutturosa*) Population." *Oryx* 31 (1997): 127–34.

Mallon, David. "The Snow Leopard, *Panthera uncia,* in Mongolia." *Int. Ped. Book of Snow Leopards* 4 (1984): 3–9.

Man, John. *Gobi.* London: Weidenfeld and Nicolson, 1997.

McCarthy, Thomas Michael. "Ecology and Conservation of Snow Leopards, Gobi Brown Bears, and Wild Bactrian Camels in Mongolia." Ph.D. Diss., University of Massachusetts, Amherst, 2000.

McCarthy, Thomas, Todd Fuller, and Bariusha Munkhtsog. "Movements and Activities of Snow Leopards in Southwestern Mongolia." *Biological Conservation* 124 (2005): 527–37.

McCarthy, Thomas, and David Mallon, eds. *Snow Leopards.* London: Academic Press, 2016.

McCarthy, Thomas, Lisette Waits, and Batmukh Mijiddorj. "Status of the Gobi Bear in Mongolia as Determined by Noninvasive Genetic Methods." *Ursus* 2, no. 1 (2009): 30–38.

Mueller, Thomas, Kirk A. Olson, Todd K. Fuller, et al. "In Search of Forage: Predicting Dynamic Habitats of Mongolian Gazelles Using Satellite-based Estimates of Vegetation Productivity." *Journal of Applied Ecology* 45 (2008): 649–58.

National Research Council. *Grasslands and Grassland Sciences in Northern China.* Washington, D.C.: National Academy Press, 1992.

Odonkhuu, Daria, Kirk A. Olson, George B. Schaller, et al. "Activity, Movements, and Sociality of Newborn Mongolian Gazelle Calves in the Eastern Steppe." *Acta Theriologica* 54, no. 4 (2009): 357–62.

Olson, Kirk A. "Ecology and Conservation of Mongolian Gazelle (*Procapra gutturosa* Pallas 1777) in Mongolia." Ph.D. Diss., University of Massachusetts, Amherst, 2008.

Olson, Kirk A., and Todd K. Fuller. "Wildlife Hunting in Eastern Mongolia: Economic and Demographic Factors Influencing Hunting Behavior of Herding Households." *Mongolian Journal of Biological Science* 15, no. 1 (2017): 37–46.

Olson, Kirk A., Todd K. Fuller, Thomas Mueller, et al. "Annual Movements of Mongolian Gazelles: Nomads in the Eastern Steppe." *Journal of Arid Environments* 74 (2010): 1435–42. doi:10.1016/j.jaridenv.2010.05.022.

Olson, Kirk A., Todd K. Fuller, George Schaller, et al. "Estimating the Population Density of Mongolian Gazelles *Procapra gutturosa* by Driving Long-distance Transects." *Oryx* 39, no. 2 (2005): 164–69.

Olson, Kirk A., Todd K. Fuller, George Schaller, et al. "Reproduction, Neonatal Weights, and First-year Survival of Mongolian Gazelles (*Procapra gutturosa*)." *Journal of Zoology* 265 (2005): 227–33.

Olson, Kirk A., Elise Larsen, Thomas Mueller, et al. "Survival Probabilities of Adult Mongolian Gazelles." *Journal of Wildlife Management* 78, no. 1 (2013): 1–8.

Olson, Kirk A., George Schaller, L. Myagmasuren, et al. "Status of Ungulates in Numrug Strictly Protected Area." *Mongolian Journal of Biological Sciences* 2, no. 1 (2004): 51–53.

Owen, Stephen. *The Great Age of Chinese Poetry: The High T'ang.* New Haven: Yale University Press, 1981. The Li Bai poem in Chapter 3 is quoted from this source.

Przhevalsky [Przewalski], Colonel N. [Nikolay]. *From Kulja, Across the Tian Shan to Lob-Nor.* Trans. E. Delmar Morgan. London: Sampson, Low, Marston, Searle and Rivington, 1879.

Reading, Richard, Sukhiin Amgalanbaatar, and Ganchimeg Wingard. "Argali Sheep Conservation and Research Activities in Mongolia." *Open Country* 3 (Fall 2001): 25–32.

Reading, Richard, Dulamtserengiin Enkhbileg, and Tuvdendorjiin Galbaatar, eds. *Ecology and Conservation of Wild Bactrian Camels* (Camelus bactrianus ferus). Ulaan Baatar: Mongolian Conservation Coalition, 2002.

Reading, Richard, Henry Mix, Badanjavin Lhagvasuren, and Evan Blumer. "Status of Wild Bactrian Camels and Other Large Ungulates in Southwestern Mongolia." *Oryx* 33, no. 3 (1999): 247–55.

Rivals, Florent, Nikos Solounias, and George Schaller. "Diet of Mongolian Gazelles and Tibetan Antelopes from Steppe Habitats Using Premaxillary Shape, Tooth Mesowear and Microwear Analysis." *Mammalian Biology* 76 (2011): 358–64.

Rotshild, E. V. "Infectious Disease as Viewed by a Naturalist." *Open Country* 3 (Fall 2001): 46–62.

Schaller, George. "On Meeting a Snow Leopard." *Animal Kingdom* 75, no. 1 (1972): 7–13.

Schaller, George. *Tibet Wild.* Washington, D.C.: Island Press, 2012.

Schaller, George. *Wildlife of the Tibetan Steppe.* Chicago: University of Chicago Press, 1998.

Schaller, George, and Badamjavin Lhagvasuren. "A Disease Outbreak in Mongolian Gazelles." *Gnusletter* (IUCN) 17, no. 2 (1998): 17–18.

Schaller, George, Jachliin Tserendeleg, and Gol Amarsanaa. "Observations on Snow Leopards in Mongolia." In *Proceedings of the Seventh International Snow Leopard Symposium,* 33–42. Seattle, Wash.: International Snow Leopard Trust, 1994.

Schaller, George, Ravdangiin Tulgat, and B. Navantsatsvalt. "Observations on the Gobi Brown Bear in Mongolia." *Moscow: Bears of Russia and Adjacent Countries — Status of Populations; Proceedings of the Sixth Conference of Specialists,* 1993. Vol. 2, pp. 110–123.

Scharf, Katie M., Maria E. Fernandez-Gimenez, Batjav Batbuyan, and Sumiya Enkhbold. "Herders and Hunters in a Transitional Economy: The Challenges of Wildlife and Rangeland Management in Post-Socialist Mongolia." In *Wild Rangelands,* ed. Johan DuToit, Richard Kock, and James Deutsch, 312–339. Oxford: Wiley-Blackwell, 2010.

Sergelenkhuu, Jambal, and Batlai Oyuntseseg. *Flowers of Hustai National Park.* Ulaanbaatar: Selenge Press, 2014.

Stubbe, Annegret, ed. *Exploration into the Biological Resources of Mongolia.* Vols. 10; 16. Halle/Saale, Germany. Martin-Luther-Universität Halle-Wittenberg, 2007; 2016.

Suttie, J. M., and S. G. Reynolds, eds. *Transhumant Grazing Systems in Temperate Asia.* Rome: FAO, 2003.

Townsend, Susan E., and Peter Zahler. "Mongolian Marmot Crisis: Status of the Siberian Marmot in the Eastern Steppe." *Mongolian Journal of Biological Sciences* 4, no. 1 (2006): 35–43.

Tulgat, Ravdanjiin, and George Schaller. "Status and Distribution of Wild Bactrian Camels *Camelus bactrianus ferus. Biological Conservation* 62 (1992): 11–19.

Wingard, James, and Peter Zahler. *Silent Steppe: The Illegal Wildlife Trade Crisis in Mongolia.* Washington, D.C.: East Asia and Pacific Environment and Social Development Department of the World Bank, 2006.

Wang, Xiaoming, Helin Sheng, Junghui Bi, and Ming Li. "Recent History and Status of the Mongolian Gazelle in Inner Mongolia, China," *Oryx* 31, no. 2 (1997): 120–26.

Zahler, Peter, Kirk A. Olson, George Schaller, et al. "Management of Mongolian Gazelles as a Sustainable Resource." *Mongolian Journal of Biological Sciences* 1 (2003): 48–55.

Zhirnov, L. V., and V. O. Ilyinsky. *The Great Gobi National Park: A Refuge for Rare Animals of the Central Asian Deserts.* Moscow: USSR/UNDP Project, Centre for International Projects, GKNT, 1986.

Acknowledgments

During my many journeys to Mongolia between 1989 and 2007 to collaborate on wildlife and conservation issues, I received valued help and cooperation from several institutions and many individuals. Most of these are mentioned in the text, and they are also indicated in our joint publications listed at the end of the book. As a staff field biologist with the Wildlife Conservation Society in New York, I worked in Mongolia under its auspices. I owe a special debt to Jachliin Tserendeleg, of the Mongolian Society for Environment and Nature, who was an inspiration to me with his constant interest in and contributions to our work. His death in 2001 deprived not only us of a friend and colleague but Mongolia of one of its most dedicated conservationists. The Ministry of Nature and Environment, the Mongolian Academy of Sciences, the National University of Mongolia, and the Great Gobi National Park Administration each made important contributions to our project. I am especially grateful to Minister for Nature and the Environment Zamba Batjargal for his valuable assistance, and also wish to express my admiration for his dedication to conservation. The United Nations Development Programme under its Global Environmental Facility's Eastern Steppe Biodiversity Project enabled many Mongolian and foreign researchers to be afield, including myself. Several institutions assisted us by analyzing specimens and evaluating data. These include the Department of Animal Science of Cornell University, the Field Veterinary Program of the Wildlife Conservation Society, and the Conservation and Research Center of the Smithsonian Institution.

Herder households offered us help and hospitality with shelter and food, no matter the time of day, the season, or the weather. Their goodwill is one of my fondest memories of Mongolia.

Many individuals provided valuable assistance in the field, most of them Mongolians but also Russians, Australians, and North Americans. Badamjavin Lhagvasuren, Ravdangiin Tulgat, and Daria Odonkhuu among Mongolian colleagues deserve special mention. My wife, Kay, ably assisted on several trips. Thomas McCarthy and Kirk Olson each devoted years to Mongolian wildlife, and the latter retains his devotion to the country by living there.

I extend my appreciation to all individuals and institutions for their valuable contributions to this project and to Mongolia's environment.

I also express my deep gratitude to Beth Wald for preparing the maps. I further thank the two reviewers of the manuscript for their comments and Michael Deneen and Susan Laity of Yale University Press for their excellent editorial assistance.

Index

Page numbers in italics indicate photographs and maps.